"*The Ultimate Speaker's Guide* is a comprehensive guide to ~~~~ ~ ~~~~ ~ ~~
or advancing a speaking career. Kathy Carlton Willis poured herself
and her years of experience and expertise into this book. It is the best
book I've seen for both speaker-wannabes/oughta-bes and frequent-fly-
ing pros. Kathy's spiritual depth and integrity offer helpful balance to
the very me-centered industry of building and expanding a platform.
She shares with generous abandon from her years in the industry and
possibly has written herself out of a job with this book. The clean, bul-
let-point style and good illustrations make for an easy read. *The Ultimate
Speaker's Guide* removes all excuses for speakers who want to plunge into
speaking, professionalize their platform, or expand their reach."

– **Jane Rubietta**, Platform and Book Coach, Author,
International Speaker

"Kathy Carlton Willis is a gifted communicator. In *The Ultimate
Speaker's Guide*, she shares many of the tools that have worked for her
throughout her career. Her passion to help others is obvious in all that
you read. Whether you are a new speaker, just starting out, or someone
who has been speaking for years, I encourage you to take advantage of
Kathy's wisdom and experience. You won't be sorry. I am proud to call
Kathy a trainer for our CLASS Staff, teaching others to be all that God
has called them to be."

– **Florence Littauer**, International Speaker, Author (known for
her books on the personalities) Founder of CLASSEMINARS
(Christian Leaders, Authors and Speakers Seminars)

"Whether you're a beginner or a seasoned professional, *The Ultimate
Speaker's Guide* is a MUST resource for all speakers! I love that Kathy
covers it all—the spiritual and the practical—from discerning God's call,
to honing your craft, to branding and creating a platform. This book is
a rich toolkit of resources you will turn to again and again. It's already
become my go-to guide. It's like having Kathy as your personal coach!"

– **Nancy Stafford**, Actress ("Matlock"), Speaker
Author of *The Wonder of His Love: A Journey into the Heart
of God* and *Beauty by the Book: Seeing Yourself as God Sees You*

"Whether you are beginning to speak or a seasoned speaker, *The Ultimate Speaker's Guide* is a book that you need to read and reference often. Kathy Carlton Willis has packed this title with valuable information. The book is targeted specifically to Christian speakers, yet every speaker will gain insights in these pages. As you read this book, keep your highlighter and post-it tabs handy so you can return to it over and over and glean the wisdom in these pages. I highly recommend this well-written title."

— **W. Terry Whalin**, Bestselling author of over 60 books
www.terrywhalin.com

"From first page to last, beginning with the need for prayer and ending with a vast index of speaker helps, Kathy Carlton Willis' *The Ultimate Speaker's Guide* covers all those questions aspiring speakers need to ask. Want to know how to put together a program? It's in there. Need to increase your bookings? It's in there. Want to learn how to create a contract or pack your suitcase or deal with challenges? Yes, it's all in there. A must-have toolkit for speakers!"

— **Vonda Skelton**, Speaker and Author, Founder of
Christian Communicators Conference

"I've learned great speaker tips from Kathy Carlton Willis for years and trust her sound advice. Kathy has offered everything any speaker needs for a successful career. Zip over to your favorite bookstore or web-store to order this book immediately! You'll be glad you did."

— **Edna Ellison**, Ph.D., Author of 29 books, Co-Author of
Called to Write: 7 Principles to Become a Writer on Mission
www.ednaellison.com

"Want to share God's truth, tell your stories, encourage audiences? Then this is the book for you! In *The Ultimate Speaker's Guide*, Kathy Carlton Willis offers creative and solid guidelines for new speakers striving to create their ministries or veteran speakers seeking a tune-up for their platforms. I wish this book had been available when I started speaking years ago."

— **Sandra P. Aldrich**, International Speaker and Award-winning
Author, Former Senior Editor of Focus on the Family

"Kathy Carlton Willis wrote the book on speaking—literally. As a writer and speaker, I'm often confronted with questions about protocol, promotion, and purpose. These are often questions you can't quickly Google for an answer. This is why I'm so glad my friend Kathy Willis, a seasoned communicator, has written a comprehensive guide for speakers, whether you're an emerging speaker or a career professional. This is one reference book all Christian communicators need on their shelves. Make the investment today and this book will help you improve your God-given ministry of speaking."

> – **Daniel Darling**, Author of several books including
> *Activist Faith, Real,* and *iFaith,* VP for Communications for
> the Ethics and Religious Liberty Commission of the SBC

"For years I've watched Kathy Carlton Willis in action as a speaker and as a speaker's coach through her communications company, and I've admired her creativity, professionalism, and excellent advice. Now I'm thrilled that she's made her wisdom, insight, and abundant ideas and tips available to even more communicators through her book *The Ultimate Speaker's Guide.* What a gift for those of us who speak! I plan to keep this toolkit of resources at the top of my pile to refer to again and again. I'm thankful for Kathy and know you will be, too."

> – **Twila Belk** (aka The Gotta Tell Somebody Gal)
> Speaker/Author, including *Raindrops from Heaven: Gentle
> Reminders of God's Power, Presence and Purpose,* and
> *The Power to Be: Be Still, Be Grateful, Be Strong, Be Courageous*

"Kathy Carlton Willis' *The Ultimate Speaker's Guide* is a must have on every speaker's bookshelf. By the end of this book there will be no question as to the best way to proceed with a speaking career. Willis includes tips on every subject related to speaking and provides instructions to apply those tips to your speaking career. Whether a new speaker or a seasoned one, you will learn from the expertise of Kathy Carlton Willis found in *The Ultimate Speaker's Guide.*"

> – **Linda Gilden**, Author, Speaker, Writing Coach, Writers'
> Conference Director, Co-Author of *Called to Write: 7 Principles
> to Become a Writer on Mission* and other books

"Whether you're new to speaking to promote the message God has given you or have been doing it for a while, you'll find a wealth of practical help in *The Ultimate Speaker's Guide*. Kathy's experience as a speaker and trainer fills a void in resources for Christian speakers."

— **Lin Johnson**, Write-to-Publish Conference Director
Managing Editor of *Christian Communicator*

"Kathy Carlton Willis is a seasoned pro with over thirty years of experience in the communications industry. In her latest book, *The Ultimate Speaker's Guide*, Kathy shares invaluable techniques based on this personal experience. The book is filled with up-to-date resources to equip and encourage communicators. Whether you are just starting out or you are a veteran speaker, there's something for you. You will find practical new tools to establish, enhance, or expand your speaking platform. Kathy serves on the CLASSEMINAR staff and is a frequent faculty member at the CLASS Christian Writers Conference. The information in this book is sure to ignite your passion for speaking and provide you with all you need to accomplish your goals."

— **Gerry Wakeland**, President, CLASSEMINARS, Inc., Speaker
and Church Ministry Staff Encourager, Mentor and Trainer

"Today, it's not enough for a speaker to be an impressive orator, who can craft compelling presentations and deliver them with great aplomb. Knowing this, Kathy has written *The Ultimate Speaker's Guide*, addressing everything from the initial idea of becoming a speaker to all that is required to establish and run a thriving business, capable of successfully utilizing the Internet and media for marketing and promotion. *The Ultimate Speaker's Guide* offers more vital information and practical help than I've seen in any other single resource in my over twenty years speaking. Speakers at any level of experience who read this book will find invaluable information to enhance and extend their platform."

— **Pamela Christian**, Speaker, Media Personality,
Known as "the faith doctor," Author of
Examine Your Faith and other books

The Grin Gal's Guide to Public Speaking

THE ULTIMATE SPEAKER'S GUIDE

Practical Tips, Tools & Takeaways

Kathy Carlton Willis

3G BOOKS

The Ultimate Speaker's Guide
Practical Tips, Tools & Takeaways
©2019 by Kathy Carlton Willis
www.kathycarltonwillis.com

ISBN 978-1-7330728-0-9

Published by 3G Books, Beaumont, TX 77706
www.threegbooks.com.

Portions of this book were previously published in *Speaker to Speaker: The Essential Speaker's Companion* by Kathy Carlton Willis. Content has been extensively revised and updated, with 50% new content added for this release.

Edited by Virginia Smith (previous edition) and Robin Steinweg
Copyediting by Marcia Hornok (previous edition)

Interior and Cover Design by Michelle Rayburn
www.missionandmedia.com

Table of Contents

SECTION TWO
Speaking Craft–Working Up Your Program

SECTION THREE
Speaking Customized–Dreaming Up Your Niche

SECTION FOUR
Speaking Challenges–Smoothing Out Your Rough Spots

SECTION FIVE
Speaking Checklists–Lining Up Your Resources

SECTION SIX
Speaker Conundrums–Answering Questions

SECTION SEVEN
Special Commission–Sending Up a Prayer

Introduction

Did you ever wish you had a personal coach to equip you with all the essentials you need to take your public speaking to the next step? No matter if you're just starting out or if you're a seasoned speaker, with all the changes in the industry you could probably use a companion to help grow your ministry or business. *The Ultimate Speaker's Guide* comes from a lifetime of coaching communicators to hone their craft and develop their public speaking businesses. Most of this book stems from conversations we've had over the past couple of decades.

Can you list your favorite speakers? You can learn insights for your own speaking career by evaluating the unique abilities of your speaking role models. Some of the speakers who impacted and shaped my own public speaking (past or present), and their strengths are:

- Dr. Norma Gillming (grace and grit)
- Liz Curtis Higgs (encouraging and edifying)
- Paula Dunn Egel (uplifting and up-looking)
- Dr. Jerry Falwell (confidence and charisma)
- Thelma Wells (buzz and boldness)
- Sandra Aldrich (humility and hilarity)
- Babbie Mason (hope and home)

In my own speaking career I'd like to spotlight a couple of landmark influencers.

Dr. Norma Gillming established such a deep impression as a public speaker in my early adult years, that even though I've been blessed to hear high-profile speakers all over the country, none have replaced her as my number one role model. What about her stands out?

- Grace-filled and gracious
- Welcoming and warm-spirited
- Brilliant instructor
- Adept humor delivery
- Inspirational faith-walk

Mrs. Gillming taught me how to exude confidence on stage while also oozing humility. It's part posture, part attitude, but mostly being open as an instrument for God's use.

Later, another speaking mentor came into my life. I met Betty Southard in person for the first time at a CLASS Christian Writers Conference where we were both on faculty. After that conference CLASSEMINARS invited me to join their training staff. But first I had to undergo the same training I'd be offering others. Having Betty Southard as my coach for the seminar was a significant turning point in my life. Betty gave me positive critiques, spotlighted my strengths, and brainstormed what I needed to move to the next level. She gave me a vote of confidence as we discussed my speaking goals. I'll never forget her first words after my last presentation: "Well there's no doubt you can speak, Kathy—you're a natural. I can't think of anything to pick apart, but let's talk about some of your strong points." She believed in me. And that investment of time upgraded my public speaking career. Thank you, Betty!

A Guide for Your Guide

When shoppers go into a supermarket, they make a list or have in mind what they need. Some shop just enough for one meal. They grab a handheld basket to quickly navigate the store for only a few items. Other shoppers intend to buy enough to feed their family for a month—and they fill their cart (called a buggy in the South).

As you read *The Ultimate Speaker's Guide*, decide if you need a basket or a buggy. Don't let the ideas (the grocery choices) overwhelm you. Make a list, take what you want, and know that the rest will be there when you need it.

The Ultimate Speaker's Guide is designed to be a toolkit of resources, so use the tips, tools and takeaways as you see fit. You can read straight through or choose the sections you want to read—when you want to read them. Refer to the book often as you develop your speaking business. You might come across ideas or terminology which is unfamiliar. I've included a glossary in the back to help you. Research new ideas from this book by consulting outside resources to help you get to the next stage of your speaking career. I'm also available for one-hour consultations.

Ask God to give you the dreams he has for you in the field of public speaking. He'll help shape your vision, craft your words, and open doors for your gigs. Let him be your manager and you'll never go wrong.

Sweet Words

I look forward to hearing how you take care of business for your speaking career. One way to keep it all in focus is to be mindful of Psalm 19:14, "May the words of my mouth and the meditation of my heart be pleasing to you, O Lord, my rock and my redeemer."

SECTION ONE

SPEAKING CAREER
Setting Up Your Business

PRAYER: YOUR BEST SPEAKER RESOURCE

Often, we set up our speaking ministry backwards. We get invited to speak the first time, decide we like it, and go about trying to become an established speaker. We get a website, send out mailers, and do what we can to spread the word. We wait to organize the prayer aspect of our ministry until we think we have arrived. When I suggest that a new speaker set up a prayer team, they often ask me, "Isn't it too soon? Won't the ones I ask to be on my team think I'm acting like a diva when really I'm just a nobody?"

When we delay or omit prayer as a foundational element of our speaking careers, we miss out on the best speaker resource available to Christians. God doesn't want to merely bless what we ask him to bless, he wants to be the one orchestrating each move. Prayer assures that.

Prayer Starts with You

Don't ask God to join your efforts, ask him to lead. Yield to his direction and he will show you the wisdom you need to set up each part of your speaking ministry: the messages, the mailers, and the methods.

Setting up a Prayer Team

I believe it delights God to listen to and answer prayers, so I set up intentional opportunities to talk to him. I request his attention on behalf of each task, each burden, each opportunity. He opens and closes doors. He equips. He connects those who need to know each other. He makes good stuff happen!

So, rather than saying I believe in the power of prayer, I say I believe in the power of the object of our prayers—God Almighty. Prayer taps in to his power in a special way, especially when we seek God on behalf of each other rather than only for our own needs. Often God will nudge someone on the prayer team to pray and they will lift you up without knowing any details. Later you can pinpoint exactly what was happening at that moment. There will be times God's peace is accented in a special way, and you'll discover someone on your prayer team prayed for peace. Who doesn't need peace?

That said, it's never too early to set up a prayer team. How do you select individuals? I have found it's best to collect names from every aspect of your life—not merely others in the same industry. You will be surprised who wants to invest in your prayer support.

Don't ask too many. Usually 5-25 works well. Fewer if they will also be your wisdom team and more if you'll be sending out more general prayer requests such as with a newsletter. Set it up however works for you.

Here are a variety of ideas to choose from:

- Send requests only as they come in, one at a time—and in so doing you will have a random schedule.

- Have a specific time to send prayer requests—perhaps once a month—and combine a list of several requests at one time. (Whether you send random requests only when issues surface, or if you send a regular note, be sure not to fatigue your team members with too much information. I've done that, and it's not pretty!)

- Only make requests related to your speaking and writing, unless they are also your "do life together" prayer team.

- Ask for their prayer requests and either pray individually for them or if they agree, send their requests in the same prayer note so that it's more of a family lifting up each other rather than one person in the spotlight.

- Activate the prayer team when special opportunities surface, such as book manuscripts being considered at publishing board meetings or an event planning team considering you to speak for their upcoming retreat.

- Report to the prayer team after events are over to let them know specifics of how God moved on behalf of their prayers. This will keep them pumped up!

- Recruit those who are brave and bold in their requests with God. You need a supportive team who won't become jealous of your position and who will feel invested in your ministry. They are behind the scenes getting something accomplished! If God's favor shines on you, it's often because of your prayer team.

- Pray about whom to invite. God might remind you of someone not normally on your radar. Be prepared to be blown away by what happens as you follow his direction.

- Ask each prayer member for a one-year commitment (which of course they can back out of at any time if something new comes into their lives). At the end of each year, re-evaluate who should be on the team. Some might want out, and some might not have connected in the best way. Don't feel obligated to re-invite anyone who seems distant. If you haven't set a term limit to volunteer on your team, it can become awkward for both parties.

- Give the new prayer team members an idea of what they are joining. If you need to make any changes, try to do it when you start a new year together.

Be Cautious

Don't get your feelings hurt if someone declines your invitation or leaves after having served on the team. God is the one at work shaping your team—it's not a popularity contest. Be hesitant to say yes to ones who invite themselves to serve on your team. They may have ulterior motives. I've been burned this way, especially by others in the same industry who want to duplicate my ideas and chase down my opportunities for themselves.

If someone volunteers to be on your prayer team, thank them and let them know you can't include everyone who asks. You'll let them know if there is an opening in the future. Ask God if this is a safe person for your team. Those who aren't part of your more intimate prayer team family can still pray in general for your ministry. It's essential, due to the nature of what you'll be sharing, that these prayer requests are confidential.

Event Prayer Team

Often, event leaders form prayer teams for their specific events. Speakers miss out when they don't ask if they can have interaction with this team. If the event doesn't have a prayer team formed, they might scramble to put one together because they're so excited you want to be part of the prayer support for their event.

There are several ways you can plug in to this team:

- Send them a list of your prayer requests for the event to add to their event prayer list.

- Offer to have a video call or speaker call to pray together as a team. This also serves to get them excited about the event in advance, hear your heart, and spread your passion to others before you ever get there. And best of all, God is in the middle when we gather together like that.

- Ask them for a list of those registering for the event. You and their prayer team can start praying over the names. When I was a women's ministry director, one of our speakers requested our ticket list so she could pray specifically for attendees by name prior to the event. Women wanted to buy tickets earlier than usual so they could have someone famous praying for them. They felt connected to the speaker before she arrived, simply because she showed she cared. There's nothing more precious than for a person to know you are lifting their name up to the Father—that means the world to them!

- Pray the room before the event starts. You can do this by yourself or with the prayer team. Stop and rest your hand on each seat or section as you envision who might sit there. Ask God to do a work and prepare each heart and mind before you speak the first word of your program. Surrender to his use, like empty conduit prepared to flow from the Source.

Don't Forget These Prayer Needs

- Pray for content. As you put together new speaking programs and writing content, ask your prayer team to partner in prayer with you that God will reveal the best ideas to you. Mention it on social media. Tell your church family. Share with any professional groups who have prayer loops. Don't be shy about asking for prayer when it comes to content.

- Pray for direction. This is an important time for God to be in the lead and for you to follow—not the other way around. Whenever I get ahead of God it always leads to disaster. Never fails. And when I pray first, God shows me ideas I would have never dreamed up on my own.

- Pray for results. It's never too early to ask God to use you in a way that expands the Kingdom. Even if you are a corporate speaker rather than a faith-themed speaker, if you are a believer you know it is God who brings the increase to every planting season. Make sure your motive for seeking results isn't to feed your pride but rather to make a difference in the lives of others.

- Pray for numbers. That's right—it's okay to pray for God to grow the numbers. As long as your motives are pure, God loves to show himself mighty in the numerical Miracle Grow business. Think of all the avenues where numbers are important: (1) funds, (2) event registrations, (3) ticket sales, (4) reduced expenses, (5) donations, (6) book contracts, (7) product sales, etc.

Whether you start with a prayer team or build one later in your speaking career, it's never too late or too early to have a prayer team. Activate your team as needed to bolster your ministry, and you'll use the best speaker resource of all.

THE BUSINESS OF SPEAKING

Setting up your speaking ministry to be productive and efficient takes business savvy. Trade your hobby mentality for that of a CEO and you'll be successful in your endeavors. Do a quick checkup to see if you've mastered the business mode for each of the following elements and work to eliminate any weak spots you find. I expand on these later in the book, but for now evaluate the following aspects of your speaking business.

Respectable Office

One way to ramp up your speaking career is to set up your office to function effectively. Your receptionist might simply be a business-like greeting on your voicemail's outgoing message. Many speakers work from home, so purchase supplies and software programs you might need to run your business. Consider subscribing to an e-blast server. Get a postage system for use at your home office and maintain a sharp website. Have unique print products made that reflect your brand. If you want to keep your home address private, obtain a post office box number. Comply with any laws in your municipality or county for getting a business license, and also set up a banking account for your business funds.

Regular Contracts

Do you have a speaking agreement or contract that comes from a reputable template or has been approved by a legal consultant? Speakers who have been on the circuit for long have been burned enough to realize the necessity of a binding contractual agreement. Unfortunately, some contracts read more like a Hollywood rider, complete with a shopping list of items to have in the green room. While I'm not recommending you eradicate your rider if you have one, you might want to modify it so you don't develop a diva reputation.

A basic contract should cover:

- Date and time
- Location
- Sponsor/host
- Travel expense details, transportation information, etc.
- Speaker fee and deposit
- Speaking topic, number of times to speak, length of each message
- Meal and lodging details
- Audio/visual requirements
- Resource table
- Cancellation policy

Reasonable Fees

Create a price list of your standard fees so when organizations and event planners request it, they know you aren't quoting a random rate. Specify your travel expenses, hotel and lodging as well. When you receive inquiries, ask what their customary budget is for such an event and suggest ways to increase their income on an event if it's quite a bit less than your usual fee. Of course you can offer creative booking options for those with budget restrictions, such as:

- Clustering the event with another in the same area
- Providing publicity so more registrations come in
- Charging a per person fee
- Providing each attendee with a book or product as part of the set rate
- Offering to write off part of the fee to give them a reduced honorarium rate
- Coming for travel fees only, plus donations and the opportunity to sell your products

In an upcoming chapter I will discuss speaker rates in more detail.

Requiring Deposits and Cancellation Fees

Nonrefundable deposits are standard in the speaking industry and often amount to 25-50 percent, with the remainder paid at the event. Compare a variety of cancellation clauses from speakers to select the one that best reflects your ministry and business practice.

Requesting Feedback

Some speakers provide standard survey questionnaires after events in order to gather valuable feedback from attendees. Other times, the event planners provide these evaluation forms. One way to collect their input is to ask them to place a note into a fishbowl at a table near your product table (so they don't have to stand in line to drop off their notes). Speakers improve on their weaknesses and accent their strengths when they receive input regarding what is working and what can be improved. Critiques aren't meant to tear down but to build up. Positive responses will keep you going, and constructive suggestions will help you aspire to do better next time.

Look at it this way—if the message were a prayer, the feedback from the message would be the amen. I heard it said to never allow praise to go to your head, and never allow criticism to go to your heart.

Feedback also gives you the paperwork to ask them for an endorsement or a referral for other events.

Requesting Endorsements

Each time you speak your message will impact audience members and organizational leaders. When they compliment your program, thank them and ask if they'd mind writing that very same sentiment for you to share in promotional materials. Letter-length references on official letterhead are nice to have, but even short blurbs combined together on one promo page are beneficial. Assemble quotes from leaders and attendees alike. Add their names and roles after their words of praise.

Ask for many endorsements so you can select the best ones. Some of the feedback I receive are cherished treasures because I had no idea how those high-profile individuals felt about my speaking.

Encourage endorsers to use colorful writing. Provide samples to help get them started. Request blurbs from those you know are skillful writers, but ask others too, because you might be surprised what you get back. It's fine for you to pull out key statements from several endorsements—don't feel obligated to use the entire quote if it doesn't fit what you need. File any you don't use for future purposes.

When event planners read what others think of your speaking, they won't feel they are taking such a big risk to invite you to speak. Remember, they are going to be fairly protective of their group and are hesitant to allow strangers to use their podiums unless you come with good credentials.

Resource Table

Even if you don't have a book published, request a resource table in your speaker contract. If needed, ask for someone to assist with the cash drawer so you can have more interaction with your audience. View the resource table as an opportunity to extend your ministry time with people who are taking your message home with them.

Product sales help supplement honorariums and make up for lower paying gigs. Ideally, more than half of your speaker income could come from product sales. Find a table décor that is crushable and can be packed for air travel and still look fresh. An eye-catching display will draw traffic to the table. I'll discuss more about setting up a product table in a later chapter.

Taking Care of Business

Did you find any aspects of your speaking business that need work? Develop a master plan to implement the necessary changes in the way you run your speaking career, and soon others will take notice. Stellar features and programs lead to grassroots buzz spread by word of mouth. And buzz leads to more exposure. With more exposure come new opportunities to speak.

One final guideline: When you take your business seriously, others will too.

JUMPSTART YOUR SPEAKING MINISTRY

How can you whip your speaking ministry into better shape, so you get more speaking gigs? One of the main reasons speakers miss out on bookings is because they have failed to promote themselves. They see publicity and marketing as a necessary evil and do as little as possible. Obviously, strategic promotion plays a big part in getting more exposure as a speaker. Publicity and marketing also help coordinators promote their events, so they get more results as well. Happy event coordinators equal happy speakers.

Do you want to be perceived as proficient rather than amateur? Most speakers got their start when people they knew asked them to speak at events. Word of mouth helped spread exposure to people they didn't know. If you are at that point—getting a few speaking events from planners you don't personally know—then you are ready to move to the next level in setting up a professional speaking ministry or business. Additionally, some of you want to find extra speaking opportunities as a way to grow your writer platform. So, where do you start?

Identify Passions

Find your passions—your heart-core messages. Audiences can sense when you are jazzed because the topic makes your head reel with ideas and concepts. What topics excite and energize you? Choose these. What topics dull and drain you? Avoid those. I knew a leadership-themed speaker who tried to add a program about hospitality to her repertoire to increase bookings. The presentation floundered. Audiences could tell there was no light in her eyes as she spoke. She needed to specialize in programs that fit her rather than seeking to offer popular topics. Once she selected her personal heartbeat messages, her eyes lit up again and her messages came back to life.

Package Your Programs

Think up five programs you could present if requested. You don't have to fully develop the actual messages until you receive bookings for these topics. All you need to do for now is come up with a catchy topic title and a descriptive blurb about each presentation. Be sure the blurbs are inviting and alluring. Make your programs relevant—timely and fitting for your target audiences. If you have a brand, your key messages need to fit your brand identity. Also include previous speeches that received positive feedback.

Event planners will look over your speaker portfolio to decide if any of your programs will work for their audiences.

Before the Booking

How will event planners hear about you and determine if you are a good match for their event or ministry? It is essential for you to show why you fit their needs. The more your name is out there, the more likely they are to run across it when they are seeking a speaker.

Event planners select speakers for events based on:
- Word of mouth
- Referrals
- Hearing the speaker previously
- Speakers Bureaus
- Search engines

- Reading the speaker's published pieces
- Hearing the speaker as a media guest

Are you doing all you can to maximize your name in all of these categories?

A professional website with SEO (search engine optimization) will help others find you when they search keywords that match your message, mission, and passion. On your website, include: about page, topics with blurbs, endorsements or references, and a virtual media kit page (press release, bio, JPG photos of you and your projects, and clippings from publications as well as audio and video clips from interviews or speaking engagements). Even though almost anyone can set up a website, having your own site helps validate you as a speaker. And if it is well done, it says, "This speaker is a professional." I will cover creating an effective website in a later chapter.

Determine how often you want to speak. What restrictions do you have on your schedule? Speakers with other obligations (family, outside job, ministry, etc.) have to put parameters on their availability. This helps them determine goals and limitations.

Ask these questions:

1. How often can I be away overnight to speak somewhere?
2. If the group requests a topic I've already done, can I work it into my schedule since I've already done most of the prep work?
3. If I'm limited on overnight travel, what groups can I speak to closer to home? (You might have to squeeze more in, earning less money per talk, but it will get you home to family quicker than a speaking gig farther away.)
4. How many Sundays can I miss from my church commitments?
5. What income do I hope to earn from speaking? How many bookings per month do I need to achieve this income goal?

Build Your Business

If you are just starting out, ask a group to have you speak and offer to waive the honorarium. This might be your church ladies group, your library, a civic group luncheon, or some other venue in town. Record the event so you can critique yourself (audio or video). If the program turns out polished enough, then you have a demo tape for potential event planners. If you receive compliments or positive feedback, don't be afraid to ask for an endorsement to use in getting future bookings.

Videotaping

In other sections, I mention utilizing videotapes in marketing. Here are some particulars for setting it up.

1. **Lighting.** Do you have both indirect and direct lighting to eliminate shadows?

2. **Sound.** Do you have a special recording microphone as well as a separate audio mic for house sound?

3. **Staging.** Remove anything from the stage that distracts and isn't needed such as extra music stands and mics. With permission of the event coordinator, move around potted plants and trees to frame your shot and disguise monitor speakers. Bring in additional staging to fit your theme. Work with the decorating committee on this so that they don't see you as undermining the work they've put into the event.

4. **Recorders.** If possible, use two video cameras so you have a variety of shots: close-up, full stage, and audience.

5. **Afterglow.** After the event, videotape the exit comments from attendees and event coordinators to use in a promo video.

Promote Your Speaking Ministry

Finally, you have enough information to create promotional materials. For that you need a bio, endorsements, program topics, etc. Design them in an e-blast server such as Constant Contact, MailChimp or MyEmma, and deliver via e-mail to potential organizations and event planners. This will stimulate more bookings. Also print some to distribute to contacts you have, and don't be afraid to ask others to hand out your information to groups they think would be a good fit.

What hard copy promotional materials are you using to tell others about your speaking services? Some use a one-sheet or tri-fold brochure. Others design interesting multi-fold cards with unique textures and colors—real attention grabbers. Do something with your materials that sets you apart from the rest. Does the style and message reflect your personality? It doesn't have to look like everyone else's. In fact, it shouldn't. What makes you different? Focus on your branding image in designing your brochure. Anything with your name on it needs to be sharp—not amateurish. Hire others to create these products for you if you can afford a designer/printer. If you cannot, study how to do it yourself and use a quality home office printer on quality paper. Or save it as a PDF document on a disc or thumb-drive and take it to an office supply store for economical printing.

I will cover promo kits later in this book but for now, be sure all promotional materials include: name, address, phone, fax (if you have it), e-mail, website, your logo and/or tagline, and if possible, the subjects in which you specialize or are considered an expert. It might be time to evaluate your business cards, bookmarks, postcards, letterhead, and other stationery products as well. Use every printed medium in your toolbox to promote yourself. Be consistent with your branding impression for anything leaving your office.

Enlist the Help of Others

It's like the gospel—you have to spread the word for it to do any good. And you have to get others to spread the word for you. Increase your use of social media like Instagram, Facebook, Twitter, Pinterest and LinkedIn. Ask questions of your friends/followers as you write your messages—they will feel invested in your work and they will be more hands-on in promoting you to others. Example: If you are putting together a program about dreaming big, ask your social network what one thing gets in the way of them dreaming big—tell them you might use their ideas in a speech you're putting together. They will be happy to help. Maybe it will inspire them to tell someone else about your availability as a speaker.

Every time you invest effort into your speaking business you create another ripple in promoting your work. And when it's a team effort, it doesn't seem forced. The last thing you want is a plan that manipulates others to respond to your invitation for bookings. Instead, wholesome promotion meets the needs of the ones with whom you interact. It's about giving out rather than taking in— shining the spotlight on the message rather than on the messenger.

Seek Additional Training

One way to polish your abilities and know-how so that you develop into a professional speaker is through special speaker training. Many Christian groups equip speakers. A group I founded, WordGirls, coaches Christian women in reaching their writing and speaking goals. You can also participate in a local group of Toastmasters to sharpen your craft. Not only will you learn more skills and grow your resume, but you'll also have a new network of contacts.

Network

Join speaking organizations, online discussion groups focused on your area of expertise, service groups—the sky's the limit. Share your expertise by participating with online communities and contributing meaningful input. Hang out where your intended speaking community gathers (whether in person, in print, on media or online). Genuinely get to know people and they will remember you for their next event or when they hear of a group searching for a speaker.

Look into speakers' agencies, bureaus and online listing services. Make sure they do not require an exclusive contract to represent you (because few are able to keep a speaker's calendar as full as you might like). Some do not charge, and some only charge if they arrange a confirmed booking.

Treat it as a Career

The more attention you give your dream to be a speaker, the more likely you will see your aspiration come true. If you treat it like a hobby, a hobby it will remain. If you respect it like a business, a career is born.

READY FOR A RESTART

I was on a roll with speaking gigs—right up to the day my career halted for an entire year due to medical reasons. In four weeks, I spoke fourteen times. And then…no speaking events outside of my own church for fourteen months. *Ouch!* During that time, I did manage to write four books, so I wasn't slacking while under extensive medical care, but still—I was left with no events on the calendar. There's nothing worse for a speaker than not to have any venues lined up—because those gigs create word of mouth for extra opportunities.

If you've had a life interruption, perhaps now is the time to get back on the speaking horse by lining up new gigs. Your reasons for needing to restart your speaking career might be different than mine. Perhaps your life situation changed. Family issues. Financial struggles. Moving to a new location. There are many reasons why speakers find themselves in my shoes. (And sorry to let you down, but they aren't even designer shoes!)

I'm going to bring you along for my personal brainstorming session in this section. Here are my ideas, as I worked to fill my speaking calendar. Perhaps you can use it like a checklist, or it will inspire your own work plan.

Before working the checklist, evaluate:

What needs to be done differently? Sometimes we have to change how we do things or what we do, based on what caused the speaking pause in the first place. Perhaps you won't be able to travel as often, or you have different booking requirements. For example, I allow an extra travel day so I don't get too fatigued before an event. Make a list of necessities so you don't find yourself sidelined again. And be sure to have a Plan B in case you do have to take an unexpected break, so that your event planners aren't left scrambling at the last minute. Evaluate your limitations so the next thing doesn't derail you.

What needs to be freshened up? For me, I need to perk up my speaker kit with new programs and updated bio. I had new photos taken this year, so I can redo my promotional materials with a fresh look.

What new technology is available? Technology waits for no one, so while you were on hiatus, it was advancing. Research what is currently offered that might benefit your relaunch. There are affordable new ways to raise exposure, recruit bookings, and connect with your target audience. Be willing to try one new thing. The old way may be obsolete. For example, fewer speakers are using speaker one-sheets and more are using e-kits, e-blasts, promo packets, tri-fold brochures or rack cards.

Keep in mind the Law of Inertia. An object at rest stays at rest. An object in motion stays in motion. A locomotive that stopped for a break takes more energy to get going again than the train that's chugging along. Don't worry—it might take us more effort to get back into speaking again, but it will be worth it. Hang in there! And what you produce as you kickstart your career will be better than what you had before. It will be Speaker 2.0 version, with upgrades!

My checklist:
- Update photos, website, logo, tagline, or anything else than needs freshened up.

- Record more videos to load to YouTube and Facebook Live.

- Duplicate a video clip or full video of event to send as a sample in my promo kit. (Or link to it online if it's an e-kit.)

- Write more articles. These can later be used as speaking topics. It builds my "street credit" as an expert within my brand.

- Create a new speaker promo kit, offering brand new programs.

- Send an e-blast of my new speaker promo kit to potential event planners. Monitor those who opened the mailer and have my booking agent contact them to follow up and secure the event booking.

- Let it be known on social media that I'm now scheduling for the new speaking season. Include a link to my updated speaker kit, which I will post online as a downloadable PDF.

- Contact previous hosts to see if any want to schedule me again.

- Pay for a premium membership with an online speaker database for more exposure, since the free membership resulted in bookings.

- Hire a booking agent to make follow-up calls for me, so I'm not pitching myself to event planners.

- Create a new program appropriate for corporate and civic events, utilizing my life coaching materials. A good one for first of the year is a goalsetting workshop or motivational talk. Contact groups to offer to be their meeting speaker. (Members of these groups are often influential in recommending speakers for churches and other groups.)

- Make a new media kit discussing a timely topic. Send to media database and follow up to secure bookings. (When people hear you on radio or TV it can result in speaking inquiries.)

- Cluster events around existing events. I have an event several states away, so I might as well capitalize on the paid airfare by scheduling other programs in the same area. I can delay my stay for a few days and increase my number of gigs. If the airfare changes due to new dates, have the new events pay for the additional rate.

- Develop a plan to encourage new bookings when at current events. If I was a blessing to the audience, they are my best advertising. Word of mouth still results in more events than any other way.

- Coordinate a free event in my area and invite regional event planners so they can experience one of my programs in person. Then they will be more likely to schedule an event at their locations.

- Brainstorm a list of potential influencers . . . people I will personally contact (not in bulk) and ask if they can think of at least one person to whom they will spread the word—a women's ministry leader, for instance. Give them materials to have ready to share. People are happy to do favors like this. Don't forget to follow up.

What do you need to do to get ready for your next speaking season? It's like preparing for an Open House. You need a schedule, a mailing list, goals, promotional print materials, and online exposure. Unlike the famous movie, it's not a matter of, "If you build it they will come [call]." Event planners won't pick up the phone and call us unless we do more than build a pretty website. We have to work it. And then work it some more. Then follow up. And try a different angle. Before long, we'll see the results of our labor—back in the game.

BUILDING A BETTER BIO

K eep in mind why you need a bio, and that will help you improve your existing bio. Remember who is reading it, what decision they are making based on it, and what sort of impact you want to make. What from your life do they need to see, to say *yes*?

Who Needs Your Bio?

- Event planners, considering your speaker promo for booking you to speak.
- Emcees, to introduce you as speaker or guest at events, to hook the audience.
- Magazine editors, in a query letter, considering your article for publication.
- Media representatives, in a media kit, considering you for an interview.
- Acquisitions editors, in a book proposal, considering your book for contract.
- Literary and booking agents, in consideration of representing you.

What NOT to do:

- Use the term "Amazon #1 Bestselling Author" in the first sentence. People have become leery of this term because they know of the gimmicks authors use to get this rating. Along with this, "award-winning" is fine to use if you earned a recognized award, but it's overused. Better to mention the most significant award you've won than to use that term.
- Use the term "highly sought-after speaker." I've seen speakers use this phrase who have about three speaking gigs a year. That does *not* qualify! Besides, it's so overused it has no influence anymore.
- Overuse exclamation points.
- Use a pun that comes across as corny.
- Write your bio chronologically. That means you start with something from your childhood or early adulthood and end with your current life. This doesn't hook the target because your biggest impact statement is toward the end. They've lost interest by then.
- Write in first person. It will sound amateur as if you are bragging.
- Sound like a resume. Your bio needs to have a heartbeat.
- Build to the important material—put the most outstanding statement first. Assume your first sentence will be the only information they read.
- Include irrelevant information. This only adds to the blah-blah-blah effect. Even if it's important information, if it's not relevant to the purpose of the specific bio, leave it out.
- Choose other overused words such as: top, passionate, outside-the-box, unique, blessed, anointed. These create tired bios.

6 Keys to a Great Bio

1. **Write it in third person.** To do this, imagine someone else introducing you to others. This helps you avoid the

uncomfortable hesitancy (and squirm!) you have of writing about your praiseworthy attributes.

2. **Keep it fresh.** Don't use a stale bio from a previous year. At least twice a year, or after any big life change, go through your bio file and update the information. Also customize the information for the specific request.

3. **Infuse it with your essence.** Let the reader feel like they know you. Cozy it up so it doesn't read like a list of facts. Can they see beyond your accomplishments to discover your personality and style?

4. **Use keywords.** Use unique descriptive words and convincing selling points. Think of why others need your bio and pre-answer their questions in a way that makes them want to know you and about your projects. Be sure it has a theme that ties to your brand, your topic, your heart-core passions, or some other story arc. This becomes a ribbon to connect all the words into a nice package.

5. **Make it short.** Why? Because others are more likely to read it. Why use a multitude of words if doing so guarantees it gets overlooked? Think of a time someone yammered away about so many mundane facts in a row—did you remember any of them? No. What is important to you might not matter a bit to the intended target. The whole "less is more" concept is true here. Leave them wanting to know more. If someone gives you a word count of 50 words or more for your bio, challenge yourself to make it less than that maximum number.

6. **Use creative format.** If you're writing a longer bio, consider a mixed format. Include some bullet point lists to break up the paragraphs. This helps the reader navigate the bio easier. Our eyes are accustomed to the speed-reading pace of the Web so duplicate that format in a longer bio. The reader will be able to scroll through it without their eyes glassing over!

Word Counts

Write your bio at different word counts. Start with the longest word count you need (250-500 words) and then edit it down shorter and shorter. Organize these documents into one bio file on your computer. In the document name, put the word count for the bio, so you can grab one quickly when others request a bio. Common word counts needed are:

- 25-30 (at the end of an article or devotional)
- 50-75 (on the back-cover copy of your books, press releases, interviews)
- 100 (for speaker introductions, query letters, one-sheets, guest blog posts and other more in-depth bios)
- 250-500 (for websites, blogs, book proposals and other longer bios)

Checklist of a Bio

Your bio might include some of the following elements:

- Your tagline or intended branding impression
- Author credits
- Speaker credits
- Education and advanced training
- Other prior or current interesting jobs/roles
- Affiliations and memberships
- Awards
- Ministries
- Family
- Where to find you online
- What others say about you (audiences or industry pros—not a family member or friend)
- A peek into your personal life (such as a hobby or opinion, to add personality to the bio, making it less stiff)

Have Bio—Will Travel

Always provide the event planners, hosts or emcees your bio when they first request your information. The day of the event, don't assume they still have that bio. Bring another copy to give to them at the venue in case they forgot your bio at home. One time I didn't do this, and the emcee downloaded an old bio of mine off the Internet. It missed my most important accomplishments and mentioned a cat who was no longer a part of our family.

Like anything we teach, when it comes to communication, whether written or spoken—words matter. Even your bio can be used to set you apart from the rest.

BRANDING FOR INTENTIONAL PERCEPTIONS

What's in a name? In days of old, parents named babies in a way that would be almost prophetic of what that child would become or what the child represented. We've gotten away from that tradition, but today we use branding and taglines to define people and businesses.

Branding characterizes the spirit of the speaker—our heart-core messages. We all leave an imprint on others—some of us do this in a strategic way while others leave an impression unintentionally. With that in mind—let's be deliberate with our branding!

Your Point of View

Part of branding is to be true to your point of view. Every speaker has a unique voice that has nothing to do with the way he or she sounds. Does your brand match your voice? If not, it's time to reevaluate.

New to branding? Invite about a dozen people to be in your think tank or wisdom team. Include a variety of people who know you well (event planners, ministry leaders, audience members, industry peers, loved ones). Conduct a survey. Ask them what keywords best describe your essence (as a person, in your writing, in your speaking, in your ministry, etc.). Pay attention to the common words that pop up on several lists. Try to capture those descriptive words in your brand. At the end of this chapter I've included sample questions for your survey.

Make sure your brand has a deliverable quality. Consumers have a Wii-FM mentality (What's In It For Me?). Brand combines voice, style, audience, content, tagline, logo, colors, and more. It's that overall impression you make (strategically) or leave (accidentally). Your brand helps you choose projects wisely—making sure each opportunity fits with your branding statement and purpose. It filters out good projects that may cause you to veer off course from God's direction. Branding is your ultimate business manager and promoter!

Creating Intentional Perceptions

Branding identifies the speaker and sets him or her apart from other speakers. Consider making a play on words in an old quote, phrase, jingle, brand or tagline. Take something familiar and make it fresh and new with a surprising take.

Branding might consist of:

- Tagline (reflects your essence)
- Consistent message, voice, stylization and image
- Logo graphics
- An implied promise that the consumer will consistently get a certain special something
- Communicating what you bring to the table
- Giving a specific perception to your audience

Branding results in:

- Name recognition
- Increased audience/platform
- Your audience receiving a specific perception of you
- Consumers relating to you and to your message
- Remembering you by your brand

How to Brand:

- Identify and develop: (1) purpose, (2) mission, and (3) passion
- Evaluate every aspect of your public image and make sure it matches your brand
- Ask: Does your brand grab consumers at both the heart and the mind levels?
- Make sure the logo and style are visually pleasing and not difficult to figure out

Setting and Not Straying from Your Brand

Branding is even more about defining the essence of a speaker or writer than it is defining the niche. Why is it some can write different types of books and be consistent to their brand and others seem to be disloyal to their readers by branching out? It all depends on voice. Does the voice match the brand?

I was blessed to speak with the incredible author and speaker, Liz Curtis Higgs. She was surprised that I like her branding because she's all over the place with her writing presence. Some would say there's no brand at all if it's not specific. I shared, "You often come up as an example in my marketing classes. I explain that writers don't have to declare a niche, but they need to be true to their writing essence. Even though you write fiction, nonfiction, humor, Bible studies and children's books, your voice is consistent in each work. I see and hear Liz Curtis Higgs in every piece I read by you. You have no idea what a relief that is to writers who are so confused by the industry push to get branded into just one little box."

That conversation was one of my cherished moments in the industry. I left her with this thought: "When your brand is true to your voice, that's the best brand of all because it's the imprint God wants you to leave."

Leave a Bigger Brand Impression

What branding strategy will you use to help get the word out about your speaking services? This is your branding footprint—the impression you leave behind. Once you have your tagline and branding created, develop your branding strategy. Place your branding where others can become familiar with your area of expertise. Work on internet article placement to various sites collecting free content. They allow a byline. And if they also permit a short bio, you can tell readers more about yourself. Think of branding like blowing a dandelion—you want the seeds to spread to as many places as possible.

Set yourself up as a topical expert. Offer media interviews on this topic. Find current events that tie into this subject matter and send out timely media releases and e-blasts. Producers and editors are always scrambling to find experts when something "goes down" in the news, and if they know you are informed and eloquent and most importantly, available, they will use you as their go-to gal or guy.

The more your name is recognized, the more likely event planners will develop an appetite for you to speak for their events. Craft your branding as a form of advertising that reaps long-reaching results.

Other Ways to Expand Branding

Another way to expand your branding is to write an e-book and make it available for a small price. Offer it for free as an incentive, such as signing up for your mailing list. (Be sure it follows current lead magnet guidelines and laws.) Include a bio in the e-book that tells readers about your speaking platform and current contact information. Always include more than one way to contact you in case one method fails.

You can also provide an inspirational/informational newsletter to your mailing list. Keep in mind, a value-added newsletter offers a true service and isn't merely an avenue for promotion. Increasing name recognition is a wonderful byproduct, but not the only motive.

Many speakers are experimenting with webinars, podcasts, video presentations and teleconferences. Consider offering conferences, coaching, classes, or seminars. They can be motivational or educational. Some speakers give courses or classes on location rather than via the Web. And others use a conference phone service. The more people hear your voice and read your bio, the more they connect your name to your branding. You will become the expert on the subject and a desired speaker.

Developing Taglines

Taglines are part of the branding impression. A tagline isn't a commercial jingle or a mission statement, but it has that sort of feel. It is a punchy slogan that defines your body of work. A successful tagline evokes an instant image of the one being described, succinctly leaving a positive impression. You want to pick a tagline that will be broad enough to cover the entire scope of your work but narrow enough to be unique and memorable.

Sometimes a tagline is also referred to as a strapline or a slogan. When identifying the components of a good tagline, look for three elements: (1) Does it succinctly voice your mission? (2) Does it offer the consumer a promise of what's in it for them? (3) Does it fit consistently with the rest of your branding elements (logo, book titles, speaking titles, bio, etc.)?

Make sure your tagline doesn't only define but uses pizzazz to punch up the sell-factor and make you a household commodity—at least to your identified niche-markets and target audiences.

Keep your tagline short—long ones are hard to remember. Make it catchy. And be sure your tagline holds interest for anyone beyond your mother, best friend or spouse. You don't want to leave the potential consumer going, "So what?" Use originality, humor, or drama to make your tagline memorable. Some use puns well; others use puns in a tired, corny way. Know the difference if you try this technique. Taglines offer a quick snapshot of what your heart looks like. If you want them to get to know you, show them your tagline, not your sixth-grade photo!

A tagline will build your public exposure, your name recognition, and even give an implied promise that the consumer will get a certain special something consistently from you. The tagline will hook your target audience because it's relevant, real, and fits the consumer's need or want.

If your tagline defines you, defines your work, and grabs readers' hearts and minds—then you've developed the right tagline.

Example of Tagline Development

When I came up with James Pence's tagline, it was so right we knew it instantly. Jim writes nonfiction and novels, and collaborates on others' stories. He is a chalk artist and a vocalist. He speaks and preaches. Even though he has a varied scope of work, his tagline captures all of it.

Drawing the Stories of Your Heart works for him because:

- The use of the word *drawing* is a double play—for his actual artwork, but also for the way he draws people in and paints people's stories.

- The use of the word *stories* relates to his novels as well as to the biographical works he writes for other people. And many of the songs he sings are story-songs so it works for that too.

- The use of the word *heart* helps people know that whatever he is sharing—in art, song, written word or spoken word—targets the heart even more than the head. Heartwarming. Heart-to-Heart. Heartbreaking. Heart-changing.

My branding impression is *God's Grin Gal.* This is a brand that developed over time based on feedback I received from others. They say I'm always grinning and ask how it's possible considering all the trials I've experienced. They also say I manage to give them a grin no matter what they are going through. For more serious topics it might not be a facial grin, but a grin of the heart. Saying I'm *God's* helps them know my worldview and the reason for my grin. The hope I offer in my talks. And *Gal?* I was my daddy's "little gal" and my heavenly father's little gal, too.

Your Tagline Project

Make a list of keywords that tie in to your message. Then play around with the order and combination of the keywords until something sticks. Think of it like mix-and-match, filling in the connecting words until you come up with the right tagline. It's almost like one of those slider puzzles where you have to move around the squares until it spells out the answer.

Your ultimate tagline captures your essence and gives others a clue to what they get when they invest in you. Ask yourself what is the Wii-FM component for others. This makes sure there's an implied deliverable to potential recipients or consumers and not just a brag about you. You'll know it when you land on it because your heart beats faster and your mind surges with ideas. Your very own aha moment!

Tagline Questions for Your Think Team

1. When you think of [your name here], what comes to mind?
2. Give five keywords that describe him/her.
3. What phrase best describes him/her?
4. What are his/her strongest gifts?
5. What visual images or mental pictures come to mind when you think of him/her?
6. What tagline would you use for him/her? (Capture his/her essence)
7. How has he/she made a difference to you personally? (It's likely your core traits will be mentioned by several on your think team.)
8. What makes him/her relevant for today?
9. What sets him/her apart from others—makes him/her different?

DEFINING AND EXPANDING YOUR PLATFORM

There are two sides to your platform. One is your message and the other is your audience. Whatever you do creates name recognition so that the public can find you (and wants to find you). Your branding and marketing strategy has the ultimate goal of expanded speaking opportunities—not just the number of bookings, but the size and quality of the events.

Defining Your Message

What does God want you to say as a public speaker? One way to figure it out is to answer these questions:

- On what topics am I qualified or experienced to speak?
- What topics excite me? What topics stir up my passions?
- What stories do I want to share? How do these fit with specific topics?
- What topics have I studied or researched?
- What topics fit with my brand and mission?
- What Bible verses mean something special to me? (If you are planning faith-based messages)
- What life priorities matter most?

- What life lessons have I learned?
- What aha moments have I experienced?
- What God moments have I witnessed?
- What cultural causes matter to me?
- As I pray, what topics does God lay on my heart and embed in my mind?
- How might my brand, my life experience and my mission give me a unique angle to shine the light in a new way on an old truth?

Being comfortable about your topic makes you confident as you speak. When you are passionate about your topic, your zeal will be contagious.

Defining Your Audience

Who is your audience? It's fine to speak to general audiences, but it's much easier to prepare your materials if you know the demographics of your target audience. If you don't aim the message to hit home with specific niches, it won't hit home with anyone—it will be too general to engage listeners and create aha moments.

Study demographics for extra help on this project. Keep in mind that your group will go beyond the target audience—this is merely an exercise to make sure you are hitting the mark.

- Gender
- Age range
- Income level
- Spiritual growth stage
- Education
- Life schedule
- Common interests
- Reading habits
- Spending habits
- Hobbies
- Vocations

I'll never forget one time when I had to change directions with a Bible study group because I had the demographics all wrong. My group was filled with younger women who were either new in their faith or not yet Christ followers. The class was culturally diverse, coming from many different backgrounds. Most were pulling themselves up by their bootstraps to work their way off government assistance. They were looking for answers, for fellowship, and for something more that they couldn't quite put their finger on. My lesson plan for mature women also mature in the faith was all wrong.

Create Your Image

It's vital to invest in your professional image. People shouldn't judge a book (speakers) by its cover (their image), but they do. First impressions. Your style becomes the first business card others see. If event planners have a choice between two speakers and one looks put together and one doesn't, they're going to select the one with a professional image. Why? This gives them more confidence that you will deliver a higher quality program. You won't disappoint them or let down the audience who has taken time out of their busy schedules to attend. Your image is one way to give your event planner peace of mind. Something as simple as a well-done photograph will communicate that you won't sacrifice quality when presenting a program.

Attend the event dressed to advertise your branding. Image is essential in communicating your message. How can you showcase your brand through your appearance? Look at your role models. Don't imitate them, but evaluate what works for them and what style will fit your image best.

What is involved in building your image? Do a personal inventory. When was the last time you updated the external impression you make on others? Use this checklist to evaluate your image:

- **Hairstyle and color.** When did you first get your current hairstyle? If it wasn't in this decade, then it might be time for an update. You'll be amazed at what a new 'do will do for your confidence!

- **Clothing style and fit.** Is it current, appropriate for the event, modest, and attractive? It's good to be trendy but don't try to rock too many fads at once or it will date your photos. Match classic pieces with one current trend for an eye-catching look that will last more than one season. Do the fabric colors work well with your coloring? Does the fit and style accent your best features and deemphasize those features that make you self-conscious? Are all the buttons and seams tacked down with no loose threads? Is it wrinkle-free? Have you checked for lint or dandruff?

- **Accent pieces.** Jewelry, scarves, handbags, shoes, belts and ties or no ties. This is the category where you can incorporate a trend for a pop of color that expresses your personality.

- **Branding.** Consider a special look that fits with your brand. A color palette, a style, a mood you create. Does it ring true for your brand? I tend to have a splash of aqua or teal in my photos and promotional tools to fit with my logo and branding. Be consistent. Be professional—not so quirky that others think you are trying too hard.

- **Photography.** If possible, get photos taken by a professional. I recently had a mini-session done for only $100 (including touch-ups) and I was given all the JPGs to use for a variety of purposes. If you can't afford a photo shoot, ask a friend or family member to help. Make it look professional by having a great pose, taken at a unique angle, with an interesting background and good lighting. The most important thing, no matter who takes the photo, is that it captures your essence. That special zing you have that makes you unique.

If you find your image falls short after taking this inventory, consider having a makeover. You can pay consultants to assist you or recruit a stylish friend to help you out. Have a make-up company do a skincare and glamour makeover. An independent consultant or a department store cosmetologist will usually assist customers free of charge. Some department stores also have fashion consultants to help customers purchase the right selections. In our resource section, I include an image consultant recommendation.

Create a Pinterest board on fashionable looks that appeal to you. If they draw you in, they might be right for your image—and they are likely to be attractive to others as well. Collect hairstyles, nail colors, wardrobe suggestions, you name it. Have it at your fingertips when you're ready to remake your look.

If you are overweight like me, don't wait until you are at goal weight for your makeover or photography session. Be the best you can be right now and don't worry about those extra pounds. If you are reflecting Jesus, they will notice him right away when they see you. Frame his reflection with the best professional image you can put together, and walk in his confidence that you are his beloved. Others will be drawn to that every time, no matter what the scale says.

And for those of you who have recently reinvented yourself, it's a great time to redo your image and your photos to reflect that self-renovation. Some people who have lost a great deal of weight are swimming in their previous-sized clothing. Celebrate your weight-loss with a makeover. Hair. Clothing. You name it! Look your best and then get new photos made.

It's time to get new photos taken if your transportation won't recognize you from your photo at the airport. This means no photos from a previous decade or when you weighed a different weight or had a noticeably different hairstyle. I once attended a speaking event and the keynote speaker stood next to a bigger-than-life-size photo of herself. Only one problem—it was a photo from twenty years earlier. All that served to do was make her look aged and tired. And it made the photo look quite dated. Don't be ashamed of the you you are right now!

DEVELOPING YOUR SPEAKING TOPICS

One of the first questions event coordinators ask is if they can look over our speaker portfolios. They want to see our most requested talks and look at them almost like a menu of choices. If they don't already have a custom theme, they might select one of your popular programs.

Your list can also include topics you hope to develop. There's no use writing up a stockpile of speeches until they are requested, but you can brainstorm the name of the presentation and the descriptive blurb, to include in your speaker portfolio. Then, when an event requests that program, you can flesh out the notes.

How do you come up with your repertoire? Start by evaluating your heart-core passions. Your topics will align with your branding. They will fulfill your mission and purpose. And they will meet the needs of your target audience.

Do you write? If so, which writings will work as potential presentations? The blog articles that received the most comments from readers turned into popular messages for me—it was a natural fit.

Often, inspiration is a key ingredient to developing your menu of topics. Before you do anything, ask for wisdom from

God. Then brainstorm ideas (good and bad) until you land on the best choices.

Next, test them out with your target audience. I use social media or online surveys to make sure these topics hit home before I finalize my portfolio. It also helps make sure the title of your speech is an attention grabber.

Re-evaluate your speaking list about once a year. Remove any topics that aren't working and add new topics that fit with your evolving ministry.

Example of Brainstorming Results

Not sure how to brainstorm for your portfolio? Here's one example from my own work. My main desire for the program was to answer the question, "What are you looking for?" I wanted a fun program with wisdom and insights added as a bonus. I tossed around ideas and realized that human nature is like the Wizard of Oz characters. The older we get, the more we accumulate what we've been searching for our whole lives.

- Dorothy: Home (realizing home is in your heart, not a street address)
- Scarecrow: Brains (Wisdom and Discernment)
- Tin Woodman: Heart (Compassion)
- Cowardly Lion: Courage

Then I put my life observation on Facebook to see what sort of interaction I might get. I posted:

> I just realized why I anticipate the 50s to be such a great decade for me . . . I have accumulated in life the very things the Wizard of Oz characters searched for. In the 50s, we've finally found these, simply by living life. Sure, we need to keep growing—we haven't attained all we can learn, but in the 50s we are more secure when it comes to finding: brains (wisdom & discernment), heart (compassion), courage, and best of all, *home* (realizing home is in your heart, not a street address).

This observation struck a chord with my contacts and there was a good bit of conversation. One of the respondents put:

> *What an interesting way to look at it! I would add something about the unexpected adventures making the journey even more interesting . . . even if you have to watch out for flying monkeys.*

Social media interaction can test not only the validity and fit of a concept, but also develop the concept with more layers and depth by brainstorming with your network.

One of the great things about this Wizard of Oz program is that the event planners will have fun decorating for it. There's plenty of material not only for the message, but also games, skits, music—the whole package.

How Many Topics?

New speakers ask me if it's okay to offer only one topic. I think it's okay to specialize in a certain theme, but within that specialty you still need choices for the host to consider. Most event planners would be concerned to think they are inviting a speaker who only has one program worked up—it gives the appearance that they are getting an amateur rather than a professional. If you are new to speaking, come up with a few potential titles for your presentations, and write descriptive blurbs, so the host has something from which they can select the best fit. People like having choices!

For print materials, a list often looks better if it has an odd number of items, so five programs is a good number to offer. But when there is no limit to space you might grow that number to a dozen. Any more than that and you'll need to have subcategories; otherwise the event planner will be overwhelmed by the choices.

Get your speaker portfolio together and you'll be prepared for the next time you get asked, "What do you speak on?"

WRITING YOUR SPEAKING PROGRAM BLURBS

While coaching a new speaker recently, I suggested she come up with titles and descriptive blurbs for her speaking programs. She wasn't sure where to start. Here are my recommendations.

What is the purpose for titles and speaker blurbs? We want them to appeal to potential event planners, so they book us as speakers. These titles/blurbs are also used in the promotional materials for the event, so they should provide enough information to attract attendees. Everyone is so busy we have to give them a good reason to come. We compete with a variety of events. Not to mention the same event might have several different breakout sessions at the same time so you're even competing with other sessions at the same venue.

Ask yourself, how will this program:

- Encourage the audience?
- Enlighten the audience?
- Equip the audience?

Make sure the program addresses a felt need. When it is finished, how will the audience think and feel, and what will they want to do, based on your information, inspiration and motivation?

Your title needs to be catchy enough to hook the target. Don't be so vague that the audience has no clue what's in it for them. Make it short enough to be memorable.

Your Program Blurbs

The program blurb is a description of your presentation, so the audience knows what you're going to cover. Set up why the information is needful. Show them how you will present a unique angle. And make sure they know what the primary takeaway is. That's what is called the deliverable. Identify the premise and the promise of the program. Don't exaggerate their takeaway or you'll under-deliver and they will be disappointed.

The blurb needs to be compelling, convincing, and confident. It should reflect the same mood and personality as the presentation will have. Is it lighthearted? Serious? Intellectual? Whimsical?

If your speaking presentation is based on a book you're writing or have written, look to the book for succinct wording. You might find it in the synopsis or back-cover copy, or in the introduction.

If your program is inspired by an article you've written, you can get ideas from the hook paragraph, the main points, and the wrap-up statement at the end.

If you have a hard time coming up with your blurb, it's possible your speaking notes are too scattered and ambiguous. Not being able to sum it up into a promotional blurb is a good sign that you need to rework the speech to be more organized and to have a good beginning, middle, and end.

Imagine what you would tell a person if they asked what your program is about—how would you sell your presentation to a potential host? Boil it down to what's worth knowing about you and about your speech.

Be sure you deliver what you've promised when you give the presentation. I've heard many attendees grumble after choosing a breakout session based on the blurb and the class didn't have anything to do with the blurb in the program. They felt like it was bait and switch. To make sure I stay on point, I put the blurb at the top of my speaking notes and tailor the talk to what I promised to deliver.

You don't have to tell everything you know in the blurb—reserve some of it for the actual speech! It's fine to have an air of suspense and intrigue—leave something to the imagination.

Other ideas for writing your blurbs:

- Read the speech blurbs of other speakers. Determine what style best fits your own.
- Write two or three different blurbs for a presentation and ask a couple of others to help you pick which is best. Or perhaps a Frankenblurb (combine elements of several into one).
- Think about your target audience and write the blurbs with them in mind. This ensures it's not merely a general description. It will suit the specific audience.
- Use keywords that match your interests, so that it best represents you—your essence—your personality.
- Write these blurbs in third person, as if someone else is talking about your program to others.
- Avoid too much hype. If you use "selling" words, the ones reading it will bristle. They'll be looking for the, "But wait! there's more" pitch, with cynicism.
- Avoid clichés unless you write them with a fresh twist.

Samples of My Speaking Blurbs

For a Women's Event:

Grin with Grace

Sometimes in life, we have the choice to either grit our teeth in response to awkward situations, or to grin with grace. Using her trademark humor and wisdom, Kathy Carlton Willis will bring to light the hidden treasures of biblical grace. This program is based on her Bible study by the same name and will be packed with relatable real-life stories to help us think about grace in a whole new way. She also provides practical tips so we can learn to be a better instrument of grace to others. Be prepared to laugh as you relate to Kathy's transparent confessions and in the process, breathe in the grace-filled truths that will transform the way you respond to life.

For a Writers' Event:
You Can't Judge a Book By Its Cover: And other Myths about First Impressions—Busted
One of the most important aspects about working as a writer is learning how to make a good first impression. With proper planning and the right materials, you'll be prepared for any opportunity that arises. We'll cover business cards, hooks, elevator speeches, networking and other ways to make positive first impressions.

For a Webinar:
Write Marketing into the Book—And Land the Deal
If you're waiting until your book releases to market your book—think again! If you're waiting until a contract is offered—it's still too late. In this webinar, Kathy Carlton Willis teaches you how to write marketing into the book as you go along. After this session you'll be equipped with new ways to sell your book—to the publishing house and to the consumer.

Take some time to look over your current speaking presentations and brainstorm new ones you'd like to work up. Use what you've learned here to write creative program titles and speaker blurbs. You will shine as you share these polished gems when you pitch your talks to potential event planners.

HOW CAN THEY CALL UNLESS THEY'VE HEARD?

If they haven't heard about you, how will they call? And if they don't call, how will you get to share the message you have so carefully and prayerfully prepared? A big concern for speakers is how to get those calls. One necessary aspect of getting the word out is to create your promotional materials. This will include print resources and a promo kit.

Elements of a Promo-Kit

- Print materials
- Bio
- Photo(s)
- Colors and graphics that go with your brand and/or logo
- Program titles and descriptive blurbs
- Endorsements about your speaking skill, style and programs
- At least two ways they can reach you for booking information
- Where to find other info, such as: website, blog, social media, etc.
- Your tagline or branding impression

Rack Card

I like using rack cards because they let recipients see your pertinent information at a glance. These are the printed vertical cards like ones you see at hotels and the chamber in racks. They utilize high-impact graphics and layout. Typically 4 by 9 inches, they utilize high-impact graphics and layout. They're printed on the same glossy cardstock as bookmarks and postcards.

Include key points about your speaking brand—just enough to intrigue them to search for more. This helps drive traffic to your website and stimulates inquiries. The sooner you get an event planner to this stage, the more likely you'll book the event.

There are many perks to eye-catching rack cards. I like how durable they are. They don't get roughed up as much as thin paper products like one-sheets. They are convenient to be passed along to others. You can mail a rack card in a business envelope without folding. They also fit nicely in an upright cardholder. I prefer the clear Lucite ones. It gives your product table a spot of height, rather than laying them flat on the table. (A word of warning: the cardholders are fragile, so pack for traveling in bubble wrap.)

The main shortfall of rack cards is the limited space for speakers who offer a number of different programs or have lengthy endorsements. Solve these problems by making sure all the data can be found on your website. Be sure to have a lot of white space rather than crowding the information. I made the mistake of including too many words on one of my cards at a smaller font size, and you had to squint to read it!

Elements of a Rack Card

1. **Attractive photos and graphics.** The glossy texture on one or both sides of the card helps your high-resolution images shine.

2. **Memorable headlines.** Grab the attention of skim-readers by having key phrases pop out at them.

3. **Tagline.** Make sure your tagline, motto, or mission is in a prominent place.

4. **Logo.** If you have a logo, coordinate the colors of the background with the logo, your photos, and the font colors. This is your branding impression. Make the most of it.

5. **Bio.** Tell event planners why they need to know you and why they want to book you. Evaluate—does your bio capture your essence? What makes you unique or special? Why should they book you as a speaker? Some emcees will use the bio on your rack card to introduce you to the audience before your speech. Keep that in mind when you write it.

6. **Endorsements.** Provide short, convincing endorsements from others about you as a person, and about your speaking programs. Name the endorser and their role or position. (If your endorsements are too long, use a shortened version on the cards.)

7. **Contact information.** Give the recipient at least two ways to reach you. Phone (with professional voicemail greeting). E-mail address. Website. Mailing address or where you travel from (so they know what to expect in travel expenses).

8. **Social media.** Encourage them to connect with you at your social media channels.

9. **Speaking topics/blurbs.** Spotlight intriguing titles to your most popular programs, along with short descriptive blurbs. If you're just starting out, simply mention potential talks, even if you haven't presented them yet.

Use both sides of your rack card. It costs a little more, but you don't want to waste that real estate! Make sure both sides give a good first impression, since you can't be sure which side they'll see first.

Tri-Fold Brochure

If you're looking for a way to organize more text in a stylish manner, try the tri-fold brochure. It can hold more information than the rack card, still looks graphically pleasing, and also fits in a business envelope or brochure rack.

One downfall is the paper's fragility. It is often a glossy paper, not as heavy as cardstock, so the brochures don't stay in mint condition for long. Because of this, they aren't passed along to others as much as the rack card. And it's harder to file away brochures for future reference.

One-Sheet

Often we're asked to send one-sheets to event planners. When they say "one-sheet," it can encompass a wide variety of printed promotional or pitch information. One-sided or two-sided flat flyers contain all the pertinent data event planners need to consider booking you for a program. They incorporate creative page layout design to break up clusters of text, for ease of reading.

One-sheets are starting to fall out of favor because they aren't durable. It's difficult to mail them flat, and when folded, they aren't as impressive. They aren't handy to pass along but are easy to file away for future reference. They work nicely as a downloadable PDF, or one part of a speaker kit folder, but not as a stand-alone document.

E-blast

An e-blast can contain promotional information in a variety of styles, mailed in the body of an e-mail. I recommend using a professional server rather than your e-mail program's bulk mail set-up. Servers offer tracking tools to analyze page-opens and click-through statistics. I'll discuss this more when we cover newsletters.

Virtual Kit

You can make any of your promotional materials available for download on your website or a document sharing site. This cuts down on mailing costs and gives the event planner an instant look at what you offer. Save as PDF documents so that your fonts don't have to be embedded. Parties who've never heard of you can learn about your speaking when they research the internet for speakers, so it's vital your information can be found. Then the chairperson can print it out to take to their planning team meeting or forward it to others assisting in the selection process.

What Next?

- Build your mailing list by collecting e-mail addresses and/or snail mail addresses.

- Select an e-blast server for e-mail distribution of virtual materials.

- Determine if you will use a professional printer or if you will print the materials in your home office. Be aware of margins when making the design. Some printers will print to the edge (bleed) and some require a small white margin. Plan that into your layout.

- Keep printed materials with you to have available for open doors that arise through casual conversation. Make sure your influencers have copies of your promotional materials too. Influencers are your cheerleaders who help spread the word about your speaking ministry.

- Find ministry expos and denominational functions to attend. Rent a vendor booth or mingle to expand your network.

- Post an e-blast link or the URL to your virtual promo kit on your social media sites such as Facebook, Twitter, Linked-in.

- Mention your kit in your e-mail signature lines. For example: "Contact me to request my speaker promo packet," or "For speaker information, click here." Include a link to your online virtual promo kit.

- Include a speaker business card or other print materials in every piece of correspondence you mail out. You never know what word-of-mouth exposure this might stimulate to help you get a new booking.

If you've trusted word of mouth to secure speaking engagements for you, consider creating promotional materials and you'll give event planners all the answers they need at their fingertips to book you. And if you currently have subpar materials, consider revamping them to include some of these features. Look for other tips through-out the book on how to use these materials to promote your speaking programs.

FINDING NEW GIGS

Every speaker I talk to, whether they have been in the business for one week or fifty years, asks me the same thing. "How do I get more gigs?" It's like anything else about our industry, it takes work and research to schedule more events. Try one of these techniques to get more bookings.

Copycat

Look for speakers who live in your same region and speak to your target audiences. Go to their websites. Study their calendars (past and future). Research each venue and create a mailing list.

You can create an Excel spreadsheet with cells for:

- Contact person (first name, last name)
- Name of church, business or organization
- Street or P.O. Address
- City
- State
- Zip
- Phone number
- E-mail address

- Website
- Notes (I annotate which speaker previously spoke at each venue)

Design a speaker promo packet and mail or e-mail to the new venues (be sure to comply with e-mail laws). Allow them a couple of weeks to make sure the material gets to the intended party. Then plan a day of making follow-up phone calls. Offer to brainstorm event ideas with them, in consideration of a booking. Let them know you are willing to have a skype call with their planning team to customize an event. Go the extra mile, and you'll get extra bookings. Think "full service" rather than "self-serve."

Prayer Lists
Keep track of prayer requests from your speaker friends about their speaking events. Pay attention to the specific venues and add these to your mailing lists. You can learn a lot from joining several speaker groups and signing up for individuals' newsletters. And be sure you aren't only harvesting these venues, but genuinely praying for these colleagues.

Referrals
Each time you speak, ask the contact person if they can give you referrals to other potential event planners. This works for the speaker because he or she gets more contacts, and it works for the event planners because they can check with the one making the recommendation to assure a quality event.

Trade Shows
Select trade shows where your potential event planners attend. Consider a vendor table to distribute your speaker kits, or merely mix and mingle. I've attended ministry fairs designed to provide event planners with resources. Also consider Christian college alumni gatherings or denominational events where vendor tables are available. (I play a speaker demo so more than one of the five senses are stimulated.)

Say "Yes" to Free

As long as you aren't out any money, why not say "yes" to an event rather than staying at home? I've heard time and time again how God brought something big out of something little. (Sounds a lot like the five loaves and two fish.) Maybe there are only thirty-five people at the event. Too small to be worth your effort? Not if you pick up another booking from it, and the new event will have five *hundred* people attending!

The same thing goes for being willing to waive your usual honorarium for an event. If you gain several bookings by attending, you will more than recoup your lost fee. So, if you need more bookings, go back to speaking several times a year for smaller groups or smaller budgets. See what God makes of it!

Seven Quick Tips

1. **Create a catchy program.** My friend Deb DeArmond has received several bookings for the same program because it is so fun attendees spread the word to other event planners. She gets to recycle the event, get new venues, and still earn an honorarium.

2. **Switch sides.** Instead of being the guest speaker, be the host. Invite a variety of event planners to a specially-themed event. Use it as a time to honor them, or to equip them with something in which they are interested. For the cost of a meal and a night, you could line up twenty new venues.

3. **Use your words.** Gain exposure and market your speaking platform through your writing platform (articles, books, guest blog posts, etc.).

4. **Become a go-to-expert.** What's your specialty subject?

5. **Create video demos of your speaking programs.** Set up channels on Vimeo and YouTube.

6. **Assemble a bucket list.** Make a list of your top 10 or 20 dream events (within reach). Find out how they determine their speakers and follow their speaker submission

guidelines. (Ask what date they will be determining their next speaker, so you are sure to get your information to them in time.)

7. **Hang out where they hang out.** Define your target audience and mingle with them wherever they gather online and in person. Ask them about events they attend. Make sure you bring something of value to these discussions and it isn't all about milking them for information.

It's a Job

You have to put in the hours to get the results. Do the math. If you find you get 1 booking for every 10 warm contacts, and you want 25 bookings for a year, you will need to make 250 follow-up phone calls and probably 2500 cold-contact e-blasts or mailings prior to the calls to make sure they get the information before your call. Hopefully your stats have a greater return, but it's better to figure conservatively.

When you work your bookings like a job, you will be in high demand. We tend to give up too soon and miss out on the harvest.

IT'S NEWS TO ME: NEWSLETTERS

Consider growing your speaking platform with newsletters. Build your mailing lists, discover new ways to get the word out, and make plans for unique newsletters this year.

Explore Other Newsletters

Think about the newsletters you read. Most of them are e-mailers rather than printed. Take a look at the ones you open. What do you like about them? Do you share them with others? Do you explore their resources? What types of material do you read thoroughly, and which articles do you skim? When you read the subject line, what attracts you to open the e-mail?

Good newsletters are relevant—they provide value-added content. They offer readers encouragement or challenge their ways of thinking. You'll find interactive resources, such as online links, recommendations, reviews and more. Notice the creative layout and design of popular newsletters that stand out because they have the personal touch (feels like "from my heart to yours"). They don't sound like "but wait, there's more" infomercials. In addition, they spotlight guest articles from other writers, to show the newsletter isn't merely a vanity project.

What Subscribers Want

Keep your subscribers' needs in mind as you build content, and you'll grow a mailing list of contented contacts. When an article hits home with readers, they are likely to correspond with you—strengthening your relational connection with individuals on your mailing list. And better yet, they will share it with others (often through social media).

You can ensure they are pleased with your newsletter by meeting their informational needs. Offer early-bird specials not yet available to the general public. Make review copies of books available. Include video links so readers can not only see you in print, but also watch and hear you. Provide tips and tutorials—readers love resources. Showcase honors and awards you receive. Highlight your calendar with upcoming events so they can meet you in person. You can also have a prayer list or event schedule list—many recipients will support you in prayer by praying through your list. Add a personal touch as well so it isn't so slick it feels fake.

Marketing and Ministry Benefits

While it's important to keep the subscriber foremost in your mind, there are marketing benefits that naturally take care of themselves when you satisfy your readers. An effective newsletter establishes your branding imprint and expands your platform. Bloggers and newsletter editors will request popular articles to feature on their own sites or in their newsletters (it benefits them to use your work, and obviously it benefits you too). Give them the reprint wording you want them to use so they properly credit you for the work. In the article's bio, mention how they can read other enlightening articles when they sign up for your newsletter, and provide the sign-up link.

Another benefit of the newsletter is its ability to highlight your products and services by leaving a professional impression. You can conduct surveys and receive reader input for future marketing strategy. Ultimately, marketing is about building customer relationships, and a newsletter helps you do that.

Many Christian speakers have ministry in mind when they plan their newsletters. Newsletters can deliver compelling messages—articles designed to inspire, encourage and change lives. It's one more way to minister to readers in between the personal contact that takes place during speaking events. One speaker said her newsletter was like picking up where she left off at the events where she first met her mailing-list friends.

Consider the business benefits of newsletters too. They offer an inexpensive way to communicate with subscribers. E-blast mailers are about $.03 per e-mail (some are free) and printed mailers are about $1.00 per address—so it's easy to see there is a higher return on investment to use an e-blast server. Newsletters can boost sales and augment speaking opportunities. They simplify the process of interacting with followers by allowing every desired action to be one click away (e-mail links, website links, video clips, PowerPoint presentations, etc.).

Expect referrals and forwards, especially with the easy-to-use social media and e-mail share buttons. Referable content multiplies your mailing list contacts without you having to roll up your sleeves to work. Growing your scope of reach is a valuable benefit.

Do It Up Right

Make your newsletter stand out from the rest. Use a catchy subject line to increase the open rate. Create visually appealing design, utilizing graphics, photographs and artistic layout. Provide sharable content. Think about what your contacts want to read, not what you want them to know. Ask yourself, who are your readers, and what do they want to read in a newsletter?

Some speakers resist starting a newsletter because they worry about coming up with fresh content every time a new mailer is due. Brainstorm a list of article ideas you can flesh out later. Evaluate what you like about good articles found in other newsletters and use those findings to think up your own new content. Determine what questions your readers are asking and write articles to answer their questions.

Look at the topics of interest on the covers of magazines—evergreen topics that are always relevant, and hot topics that are only popular for a certain trend period. Write ahead to stockpile articles to use when you experience writer's block or have an extra-busy schedule. Consider new article ideas from reading the awareness calendars, such as "Wear Your Sneakers To Work Day." When crafting articles, use wording free of clichés or unfamiliar jargon. Also avoid exaggerations (unless used for humor) or writing in a style that would be construed as over-reaching. Readers relate to transparent content.

Consider your newsletter approach. Does it reflect your style and personality? Do your readers see you when they read your newsletter? Be sure your tagline, logo and style are prominent and memorable so your branding impression jumps off the page. Determine how often you want to communicate with your contacts. Will it be monthly? Quarterly? Yearly?

There are a few rules of thumb to keep in mind when planning your newsletter. Be consistent in your formatting. Readers want to recognize you when they see the from line in their e-mail box. And they want your subject line to be consistent each time—they need to know this is the newsletter they signed up for or they might delete it rather than open it. They can't read it from their recycle bin.

Are your photos authorized? Get legal permission to use the photography, logos, and graphics you've chosen for your newsletter. Check to see the distribution terms of service for any photos you select. At least 80 percent of your content needs to be useful information versus no more than 20 percent being promotional. Newsletters cannot read like marketing material or you will turn off your readers.

Random Tips and Ideas

1. **E-postcards.** These have a two-column layout. One to update the reader about the author and one filled with helpful information for the reader. A recipe. A top-ten list. Pull-quotes from a book you've authored. Include photos, and make sure they are in the body of an e-mail and not an

attachment. Also make a link to find it online and post the link on your social media sites.

2. **Guest writers.** When you read material written by others that would be ideal for your newsletter, request permission to use it and offer cross-promotional exposure.

3. **Auto-responders.** This is a system that automatically sends out your pre-programmed document to those who sign up for it.

4. **E-blast server.** Several reputable companies offer a variety of services to help you create and send out newsletters. Two of the ones most commonly used are Constant Contact and MailChimp.

5. **Track it!** If you have an e-blast server, you can study your open rate, click-through rate, and unsubscribe numbers. See what time of day, days of week, and subject line styles work best for your mailing list. (For me: Tuesday, Wednesday or Thursday works best, from 11 AM to 3 PM central time, using a subject line that has zero hype, but lots of "what's in it for me" appeal.)

6. **Motive.** Make sure readers don't only hear from you when you want to sell them something (a booking, a product, etc.). Show that you are giving them value and they will read before they delete. If you hear they have made a file to save your newsletters, then you know you've arrived at the right approach.

7. **Value-added.** Use encouragement, affirmation, motivation, Scripture, spiritual insights, entertainment, humor, practical tips and helpful hints, interesting facts, and relatable transparency so they don't feel they are doing life alone.

8. **Voice.** Make the voice of the newsletter match the voice (style, tone, personality) of your articles, books, and speaking events.

9. **Pre-orders.** Offer your mailing list opportunities for special promotions before they go to the general public, at special rates, such as pre-orders of books.

What to Write About

- How-to tips
- A day in the life of a _____
- Calendar/schedule of what's on your agenda
- Recycled blog posts
- A devotional or short Bible study lesson
- Contests and giveaways
- Book reviews
- Recipes
- Top-Ten lists

THE SPEAKER'S WEBSITE

Is your website working for you? Not merely appealing to you but actually working to get you more speaking gigs? If you add some of the following features to your site, it can be as effective for your speaking schedule as adding a booking agent to your team. Your website doesn't need work breaks or vacations and charges a much lower hourly rate than an assistant!

Mailing List

Does your website have a way for visitors to sign up for your mailing list? This is often found on the home page in a spot above the fold, which I speculate will soon be renamed before the scroll. This location grabs the eye before the reader has to scroll down, usually the top right corner but the top left is also okay.

It's often effective to add an incentive for readers to sign up for your mailing list. Perhaps you want to set up an automatic return mail (auto-responder) that gives them a free PDF to an article or Top-Ten list you've written. Give them something in exchange for their e-mail address. But make sure it complies with current laws.

Let them know what they are signing up for. Will you be mailing them every week? Every month? Every quarter? Will they get an actual newsletter style e-mail or will it be a blog post? What extra something might they get when they receive mailers from you? Will they be paper mailers that come in the USPS or e-blasts to their e-mail addresses?

You will learn ideas for building your mailing list in Section Five.

Booking Information

Does your website contain your booking information? Can your visitors secure you for speaking events, media interviews, and writing assignments based on the information you have posted? Is it easy to access and accurate? Are there at least two ways for them to reach you?

I've heard of several situations where communicators missed out due to being difficult to reach. One editor who needed a fast turnaround time on an article assignment gave up on contacting a writer because she only had a website contact form to fill out. She hunted down an e-mail address and was a bit grumpy from having to look for it. When she e-mailed the writer, she received a notice that the person's e-mail box was full. And there was no phone number. Needless to say, the writer missed that assignment. I've heard similar stories about speakers not being invited to speak at events and experts missing out on media interviews. It's essential not to make it difficult for people to contact you.

I like to include my cell number on my website because of my professional sounding voicemail recording. It acts like a hired receptionist to take my calls! If you leave your home number, your callers might hear a family-oriented greeting on your answering machine or voicemail. Plus if another family member answers the phone, they might not sound as professional as that pretend receptionist. So include your cell number on your website. Most people who need to contact you for speaking have a long list of recommended speakers to check out. They aren't going to hunt you down when they can move on to the next one on the list.

Media Page

What if media wants to contact you for an interview on their radio or television show? Provide them with everything they might need to know. Include these elements on your media page as well. Later I will cover what to include in your media kit. Essentially, pre-answer any questions the media might have so they don't have to work to find the answers.

News Page

If a feature article has been written about you or your books, include a clip (scan it and turn it into a PDF or JPG). If the article is archived online, include links to the actual articles (not just the home page of the site). If you include links to other sites, let the Web owner know because it might lead to cross-promotion opportunities and more traffic for you both.

Product Page

Do you sell products from the back-of-the-room table at your speaking events? Then consider selling the same products on your website (books, jewelry, journals, DVDs, CDs, etc.). Sometimes a simple PayPal account can work for accepting payments.

If you don't want to sell on your site, the other option is to include a product page to a site like amazon.com. They even have an affiliate program, so you get credit for every sale made via a link to their site. Sometimes an audience member isn't prepared to purchase your items the day of the event, but they want to go home and look you up on the Web.

Don't neglect your tax responsibilities for online and direct sales. States handle taxing differently, so make sure you're informed about the laws that govern the areas in which you operate.

Speaker Page

List all of your popular presentations along with descriptive blurbs about each program. Do you pre-answer the questions event planners have? Keep in mind the coordinator might be working with a team or committee. Be sure to have materials in downloadable PDF format so they can print to pass around at a planning meeting.

Endorsement Page

Event planners like to see if anyone else recommends you for speaking events. The higher profile the name of the endorser, the more clout it might have. The best time to ask for an endorsement is at the end of an event. When someone tells you what a good program you presented, it's not egocentric to say, "Thank you for that good feedback. Would you mind writing it down and allow me to use it as an endorsement when others request my references?"

Writing Page

Do you have a blog online? Include it on your site, rather than a remote location. Blogs are a great way to help your Web visitors get to know you better. It's often a more casual look at what makes you tick rather than the formal write-ups. Consumers are curious—they want to see what your everyday life is like. And if they relate to it, all the better! If you do not have a blog, but have written other online content, include a list of links to them.

Links to Recommended Sites

What can you offer of value to your Web guests? Much of what we can pass along includes free resources. Don't hoard them—share them with others on your site. For instance, you might include a list of links to other sites you recommend or to resources you suggest.

This is a great service. You've weeded through all the choices on the internet and come up with the best information possible on your key topics. That's a wonderful benefit to offer visitors to your site—it saves them time, and if they trust you, then you have provided a screening process that helps them. Plus, each time you recommend another site, you open the door to cross-promotion and networking with other professionals who specialize in the same topics as your interests.

Free Resources

Other free resources you can provide on your site include: articles or various downloadable writings, Top-Ten lists, recipes, how-to articles, memes, videos, podcasts, tutorials—the sky's the limit. Everything you create is a potential resource for others.

Social Media Links

You want to have two types of social media buttons on your site. The first will provide clickable icons linking the reader to your social media pages. These allow your Web followers to access you on the social media sites of your choice.

The second is the share buttons to these sites. They help others to share what you've written with their own followers. For example, if they share your blog with their Facebook friends and Twitter followers, some of their contacts might share the link with their friends, starting the domino effect I love in marketing. The new kind of word of mouth!

Tagline

Give your tagline a prominent place wherever you have a presence. One of these spots will be your website. Will I quickly identify your tagline on your website? That will help me feel like I instantly know you and what you're about. If I'm considering booking you as a speaker and I've never heard you speak, I want to know your essence—what makes your heart and mind tick—before I give you the privilege of speaking to my group. So make sure your tagline is strong and instantly noticeable on your site.

Logo and Image

Use a professional logo and color theme on your website that is consistent with your branding strategy. Avoid picking overused or difficult-to-read fonts. Your brand imprint will help your target audience connect to you more if you've selected an impression that resonates with them.

Other Services

If you offer services (editorial, mentoring, coaching, etc.), be sure you have a services page that clearly states what services you offer and how they benefit a client. Include endorsements from others who have been pleased with your services.

Questions About Your Website

- Does it have all the information a new guest is searching for?

- Does it have all the information the media needs to book you and to prep for your interview?

- Does it have all the information an event planner needs to book you as a speaker?

- Is your tagline strong enough that viewers will remember it? (Strong as a statement, and strong visually as a presence on the site.)

- Does your site provide value-added what's-in-it-for-me material for your niche markets?

- What are the intended demographics that you want to attract, and is your site doing that?

- When you Google key phrases or topics that tie in to your work, does your site come up? If not, what can you do to raise your site in the search engine ratings? At the bare minimum your name, brand, tagline, and titles of books should come up on the first page of a Google search.

- Does it have clickable images that will lead to other sites/spots/pages? And if so, are there any broken links?

- Does your site use flash, and if so, does it load quickly and add to the site? If it's a distraction or takes too long to load, viewers will grow impatient.

- Do you have downloadable print materials available such as: speaker one sheet, tri-fold, rack card, influencer sheet for books, etc.?

HOW TO SET YOUR SPEAKING RATES

One of the topics I'm asked often is how to charge when interested parties ask that awkward question, "How much are your fees?" This includes multiple aspects, so I'll cover several and you can select the fee policy that fits you best—or create a blend of ideas to match your mission.

Experience

When first starting out, your fees will be much lower than if you have a national platform and years of experience. You might begin by accepting a love offering—meaning no set fee but the group either collects money from the attendees or the event budget decides how much to contribute. Some ministries offer a minimal amount, such as $50 or a gift card. Speakers who have been on the circuit longer can easily ask $300-500. The more you speak, the more you travel, the more you might charge. Some have standard fees of $2,000 or more—way more! (But you might be surprised to learn that A-list speakers are starting to experience fewer bookings due to the economy and are reducing their rates because they want to stay booked.)

A Set Fee

Some speakers figure how much time they have spent in preparing the speech as well as in delivering it. They multiply that by how much they hope to make per hour. In addition, they figure their travel time and time spent working the event and charge a lesser hourly amount for those. If they require rebound time after an event to refresh before the next engagement, they figure that time into the equation. Then they add it up to come up with their total set fee. Others know how much they need to make per month to support their budget and divide that number by how many events they average per month.

By the Head

You might charge for events based on the number in attendance. Speakers set up this system because it's fairer to smaller venues. But it might not work for you if you realize the same amount of work is going into the smaller events. If you select this system, be sure to set it up so you aren't disappointed by the income received at smaller venues. Some modify this by saying, "If you anticipate having over 100 in attendance, I can offer to charge by the attendance number rather than a set fee." Those who have written books might include a book for each attendee as part of the cost. This works well if the event charges a ticket price.

Complicating Factors

Ask yourself these questions when setting your own fees:

- Is this event out of town, out of state, or in town?
- Will I be speaking once or multiple times?
- Will I be responsible for providing other elements of the event? (Singing, publicity, skits, games, full program, etc.)
- Will I be away overnight?
- Will it take me away from a regular commitment (such as church obligations)?

- Are they asking me to customize a new speech or are they requesting a message I've already prepared?

- Are they willing to provide benefits for me as a speaker? Some barter for getting a quality audio or video recording, or for trying out a new program or even building up their list of endorsements.

- Did the group contact me, or did I contact them? When I cluster bookings in one area, I offer discounted rates (or accept a love offering) to thank them for fitting me in.

- Am I considered a high-profile speaker? Do they recognize my name in their circles?

- Will I have a resource table to sell products at this event?

Fee Schedule

Write up a fee schedule for your standard or customary fees. List the pricing for factors you deem important. Offer a package discount if you wish. Start negotiations with your usual fees including incidentals such as travel fees, housing requirements, etc. Use an online map program to check the mileage and include that in the speaker contract. It's best not to post your fee schedule on your website so you can establish a rapport with the event planner before discussing money.

Negotiating a Fee

Another way to come up with the speaking fee is to ask the event planner what their usual budget allows. Sometimes the figure they offer is higher than you would have asked. If it's much lower than your income goal for that week, see if there's a way to adjust their starting figure to get it closer to your goal. Perhaps you can offer to put an event package together that will make it worth their while to provide a higher honorarium.

When to Adjust Your Rates

It might be time change your fees if:

- Clients tell you what you're offering is worth way more than they paid.

- Your calendar is getting full and you need to be more selective in what you're booking.

- You are invited to bigger venues with bigger budgets.

- You have developed a higher profile due to releasing a popular book, having positive exposure on media, etc.

It might be time to reduce your fees if:

- Your bookings have dried up and you need to fill your speaking calendar.

- You wish to try out a new program and need some test audiences.

- You've been out of the speaking scene for a few years and need to jump back in.

- You discover the economy can no longer support the fees you used to charge, and other speakers with similar experience have lower fees.

The Bible states in 1 Timothy 5:18 (NASB) that "the laborer is worthy of his wages." That includes speakers.

I WANT TO GET PAID!

"I want to get paid!" Does this cry sound familiar? Here are two main payment-related scenarios.

Scenario #1

"I've never set up a fee schedule for speaking. I accept whatever their budgets allot. Sometimes I only get a free meal or a gift card, although a few have surprised me with larger checks. How can I set a fee without it sounding like I'm a mercenary? *It's so awkward to talk about money.*"

Whether you've gotten paid nothing, or a little something, or an inconsistent amount, there are ways to set up your speaking ministry as more of a business. There are few other services in the business world where it gets awkward to ask for money. A person gets paid for their work. I'm not sure why we've made it difficult for speakers to ask for their usual fees.

Sample Booking Conversation

"I recently sent you a mailing [or received your name from name-of-referrer] regarding my speaking programs. You showed an interest when you clicked through on the demo links [in an e-blast you can track], so I wanted to touch base with you to see if I can answer any questions you might have. I'm booking for the next 18 months—what events do you have in that timeframe that I can fill for you? Was there a specific program that piqued your interest? [Then discuss your programs and their events.]

"You're probably wondering the details of setting this up for your group. My usual honorarium for the program you mentioned is $XXX. And my expenses would be $XXX. Would that fit in your budget? If it's a stretch, I also have ways for you to bring in more income at your event. Would that be of help to you? [Send them an article on this subject.] I also offer to cluster events in your area as a way to reduce the costs for each group. If you can introduce me to other possible event planners, we can try to work it out to spread my expenses among several groups."

Options

1. Plan your pre-booking discussion ahead of time. [See sample conversation above.]

2. Create a fee sheet to send to prospective planners along with your program information.

3. Barter with another speaker friend to close the deal for you if it's difficult to discuss your fees. Perhaps you can each offer to spend five hours one month acting as a volunteer booking agent, to call potential event planners to set up events. During this call you mention the available programs and the usual honorarium and expenses. (You would have to be able to trust each other than no gigs would get poached by the one doing the calling to take it away from the one they are calling for.)

4. Hire a booking agent. Some agents work for an hourly rate, while others get a percentage of the honorarium. This gives them the incentive to negotiate a good deal for all involved.

Scenario #2

"I negotiated the price for my honorarium prior to the event. I had a contract signed. I thought I did everything right to prevent this, but it happened anyway. They didn't pay me. How do I go about getting paid? *It's so awkward to talk about money.*"

There are a few steps you can take to retrieve your money, but it's difficult and you might decide it's not worth it or it violates your Christian principles. After you ask God to direct your decision, pray over these options or come up with your own:

1. Sometimes, God will lead you to "eat" the fee. Yes, you put a lot into the event, but sometimes we are to walk away when it doesn't work out. God will give you peace about pursuing payment or donating the program.

2. Ask your contact person why they are not able to pay according to the contract. If they say it's because of low attendance, make sure they know that you delivered everything spelled out in the contract and that it costs you the same amount of time and creativity to do that whether there are 10 people or 10,000 people. Sometimes reasoning with them is all it takes for them to do the right thing. If there was some sort of catastrophic emergency outside of their control, you might offer to write off a specific portion of the fee to help them out if they will pay the remainder.

3. If you cannot reason with them, contact someone higher up in the organization to request the payment. Write a letter on your business letterhead. Include a copy of the contract. Send it with signature required upon delivery. Report facts, not feelings.

4. If you were at the event based on the recommendation of someone else, ask them to mediate the misunderstanding for you.

5. If it's a church group, ask your pastor or their pastor to intervene, to prevent a lawsuit.

6. Take them to Christian mediation or small claims court to enforce your contract.

Ways to Prevent Non-Payment at Future Events

1. Require a nonrefundable deposit to secure the event date. (You can set up your own refund policy.) This is often one-third to one-half of the honorarium. Other times it's simply the expenses, paid upfront.

2. Include your payment policy in your contract and talk through the entire contract, including this policy so there is no question what is expected. If necessary, put a clause in the contract that addresses the consequences of non-payment, such as using a Christian mediation service.

3. Set up a per-person fee so there is no excuse about low attendance. This works well if you have product. Include a specific product (such as a book) for each attendee for a set cost per person. The venue can plan that cost into the admission price. To protect your time, you might mention a minimum number required to use this option.

4. When you get to the event, ask the event planner if you can take care of the paperwork (including getting paid) before you set up for the program so you can take off your business hat and put on your ministry hat for the rest of the event. Or take an assistant with you who will manage your resource table and have them collect the honorarium while going over the paperwork with them, so you are free to pray the room.

It's not always easy to talk about money, but being a professional means getting paid for what you do.

BRING IN MORE INCOME AND PEOPLE

One way you can make yourself desirable to event planners is to help them bring in more income and/or people to their event. Consider offering this selling point as a benefit of booking you. This also helps them increase their budget to afford your honorarium. It gives them peace of mind that you are coming alongside of them to make this a quality event. Anytime the planning of an event doesn't rest solely on the host, they are relieved and grateful to the speaker.

Here are some of the services you can offer to enhance their event:

- **Per person fee**. If you help them bring in more people than expected, you receive the benefit of increasing event revenue. It's no risk for the venue and commits you to do more to help it become a profitable event.

- **Pre-event publicity.** Offer the planning team additional materials and services to help them promote the event. Some of the items you might include are:
    - Media/promo kit.
    - Social media ads, such as Facebook Boost.

- ○ Social media event pages. Visit the page and share memes that tie in to the event. Invite nearby contacts to attend.
- ○ Media interviews.
- ○ Mp3 sound clips to promote the event.
- ○ Provide designs for flyers, which only need personalized and distributed by the host.

- **E-blast mailer.** Since I'm used to sending out e-blast mailers, it's often easier for me to send out a promotional mailer than the group's event planner. By offering to do this for the group, I've just added value to my services. I ask the planner to send me their mailing list, any additional information, and to write a personal note to the recipients. I add a program blurb, a schedule, my bio, details for registration, etc. To help them spread the word, I include share icons.

Here are some tips you can give the event planning team to maximize their event promotion. They can select the tactics that best fit their mission:

- **Publicize on websites.** Be sure to give the who, what, when, where, and why. Mention any cost and give contact information for questions.

- **Post on community calendars.** Search for radio and area online calendars. Give editors plenty of warning about your event so they have time to post the information.

- **Budget for your event.** Plan ahead to optimize your event budget. Attend your organization's annual budget meeting and ask for more than the previous year.

- **Take up a love offering.** Mention ahead of time to attendees that you will be taking up a love offering to help offset the fees of the event, on top of the admission price. Some can't donate time to help with an event, so they choose to give over and above buying a ticket.

- **Organize a fundraiser.** Consider making and selling cookbooks, having a bake sale or garage sale or some other fundraiser to help generate more money to host a bigger event.

- **Offer bring-a-friend incentives.** You can give discounts when people buy two tickets, or give another special gift or deal.

- **Reward high-ticket sellers.** Offer to allow people who sell X-amount of tickets to sit at the guest speaker's meal table. (Or go out with them before or after the event for a meal if there is no meal at the event.) Another incentive is to offer them a free ticket to the event.

- **Clear the date.** Choose a date for the event that doesn't conflict with another big event in the community. (Check with the Chamber, the radio station, and the school calendar.)

- **Create a master mailing list.** Gather as many mailing lists as possible from people and send out e-mail and postal mail about the event.

- **Invite other groups.** If this is a church event, invite other churches. If it's for an organization, invite similar organizations from surrounding towns.

- **Recruit influencers.** Influencers are those who help spread the word. Create ripples by asking your event influencers to share e-mails, graphics and e-blasts to their own mailing lists and social media pages. Give them a page of ways they can help spread the word.

- **Set up an event page**. Social media sites such as Facebook have special pages to invite people to events. This is another way to create the ripple effect because when you invite people, they can turn around and invite others.

- **Offer a video call.** Set up a video call between the speaker and the planning team or organization ahead of time to stimulate excitement.

- **Select a high-profile emcee.** Invite an emcee who has public fame and put their name on all the promotional literature. Often they will also publicize the event.

- **Ask for businesses or individuals to be event sponsors.** They might donate money for tickets to give out to scholarship recipients. Or they might "buy" a table and either bring their own guests or host it for special needs attendees. Often special sponsors will also donate door prizes or lend decorations from their stores.

- **Create a ticket sales team.** Designate a group responsible to sell tickets inside and outside the organization. This sells more tickets than having a general announcement or advertisement for people to buy tickets.

When you help the event planners with these ideas, you could reap the reward of a larger check, as well as a larger audience.

SPEAKERS' BUREAUS SPREAD THE WORD

The speaker question I hear most often is, "How do I get more gigs?" They are disappointed with their speaker calendar. Even the planners who regularly book them are cutting back with either fewer events or a reduced honorarium. This leaves speakers scrambling to try to make budget. Many speakers are diversifying to fill the gap, desiring to be used even more by the Lord in their areas of expertise or passion.

One way to increase your bookings is to grow your team. If you can bring on a booking agent willing to fill your schedule for you, that is the best option. A personal booking agent must be familiar with your programs and personality. Often they agree to a percentage arrangement, so you are not out any money until you secure the bookings.

If you can't get a booking agent, try speakers' agencies and bureaus. Some offer searchable online listings, and others have a team of agents prepared to represent you to event planners.

It's beneficial to have a representative engaging in discussions with potential event planners on your behalf. They can shine the spotlight on you in a way that isn't awkward and discuss speaker fees or honorariums in a professional manner. We all need peeps who champion us to others.

Difference Between Speakers' Agency and Bureau

Some say bureaus are non-exclusive and agencies are exclusive, but I've seen that not be the case. My observation is that bureaus tend to act more as a reception desk for your bookings—distributing information and receiving inquiries to book you as a speaker. Agencies are often more proactive, doing follow-up after distributing your customized speaker information to stimulate additional bookings on your behalf.

Most speakers' bureaus I know receive mixed reviews from their clients. Often, speakers end up with unmet expectations—partly because they start with unrealistic expectations. The best way to see what the agency or bureau has to offer is to ask questions:

- Will I be represented with a nonexclusive contract so I can be promoted by outside sources as well?

- Do you charge a booking percentage (commission taken from the honorarium)?

- Do you charge set fees in addition to the booking commission?

- What do these fees cover?

- Does the bureau/agency proactively contact potential event planners, or do you basically act as a receptionist, waiting for speaker inquiries to come to you?

- Does your contract promise a certain number of hours or contacts made to pitch me to event planners?

- What other services do you offer?

- How long have you been in business?

- How many are on your staff?

- If I send a potential event planner to your company to book my event, how am I guaranteed the planner will not receive a pitch to consider your other clients?

- What is your follow-up policy? How much will your agency handle and how much will be handed off to me for follow-up?

- How many clients does your firm represent? May I have your client list?

- How many contacts are on your mailing list? This includes: event planners, churches, and organizations.

- How often will you send out mailers (physical or e-mail) on my behalf?

- What marketing tactics do you use?

- Does the mailing list match my niche markets and target audience?

- What is the duration of this contractual agreement?

- What determines legal termination of the agreement?

Contact some of the agency's clients. Be specific with your inquiry—don't simply ask if they are pleased with the firm. They might try to limit their feedback only to positive statements unless you ask detailed questions. Ask if there have been any misunderstandings or disappointments or anything they wish they would have done differently with their contract. Get a good feel for what you should reasonably expect this agency to deliver.

Read the fine print in the contract—does anything raise concerns to you or to your attorney? If there are set fees, they should be for measurable services and materials to prevent unmet expectations. Items that can have set fees might include: creating DVDs or promotional materials, coaching, hourly services, etc. The fees to pay agents for actual bookings are often covered under a percentage if they make the booking arrangements. Online-only listings usually have a membership fee rather than a percentage fee.

Information They Need

Provide bureau-friendly promotional materials to these agencies. They need to include their own contact information so they get their cut of the fees. When you remove your booking contact information from the materials you provide them so they can use their own contact information, this improves your working relationship. They will want to use your:

- Promotional materials—print
- Promotional materials—virtual and/or online
- Demo (CD, digital or DVD)
- Links (websites, blogs, YouTube channel, social media, etc.)
- JPGS (speaker photo, book cover photos, etc.)
- Endorsements
- Speaker topics/blurbs
- Program options and fees

With the speaking industry seeing a decline in numbers of bookings as well as reduced honorariums, it's wise to consider representation from a multitude of nonexclusive agencies and bureaus. You'll find a list in our resource section as well as tips on working with publicists and agents. You will likely see an increase in scheduled events when you recruit others to spread the word about your speaking programs.

7 STEPS TO "YES"

According to marketing research, it takes seven touches, on average, to convert a cold contact into a yes response. For speakers, this *yes* materializes when you receive bookings for events. But if you are also a writer, the marketing plan works for book promotion as well. We have already covered options available to get the word out about your speaking platform, so here are the seven most likely options to achieve positive results. Implement these to expand your name recognition, extend your branding imprint, and see results.

#1-Social Media/Word of Mouth

Work to grow your contacts, content, and connecting on social media sites.

- *Contacts* are the friends and followers with whom you interact.

- *Content* is the value-added posting you provide to your contacts.

- You know you are *connecting* when there are meaningful interactions—a volley of conversation back and forth. You also know you are connecting when they share your posts with others.

- You will see more of a ripple effect (which works like word of mouth) if you provide material people want to share with others.

- Share links. Links are your friends!

- Videos are the most frequently shared posts, so get brave and post video clips.

#2-Article Placement and Guest Blogger Posts

- Write 400-word articles on your speaking topics. Offer them as free content for guest blogger posts.

- Include your bio and a link to your website to gain additional exposure.

- You can also make these articles available for church bulletin inserts, newsletter articles, etc. Anywhere editors need content in print or online.

#3-Interviews

- Take your most requested speaking topics (which often indicate the subjects for which you have the most passion), attach a breaking-news type hook, and create press releases to send to media contacts.

- Become the go-to person on topics that match your branding and speaking mission. Media outlets like knowing which experts to contact as a story breaks.

- Load your media interviews to a variety of online sites to increase exposure. Make sure to get permission from the radio host or media outlet first. Some charge a fee for the rights to their program material.

- If the interview is archived on the media outlet's site, link to it from your website, blog, newsletter and social media sites.

- See Section Five for extensive help with interviews.

#4-Audio and Video Clips

- Load audio and video clips online (YouTube, Vimeo, etc.) and link to them.

- Provide a video sample from a speaking event so prospective event planners can try before they buy. These video clips can be loaded to your website as well as to video sharing sites. Also link to these from your social media sites.

- If you have audio only, that's okay too. These can be shared digitally as mp3 files, similar to a podcast or song.

- You can use sampler demos (the highlights of a speaking program) or full-length recordings of your messages.

#5-Cross-Promotion

- What other thought-leaders are reaching your audience? Contact them to see about cross-promotional opportunities.

- Share links, resources, reviews, and endorsements.

- Offer to sell their products at your resource table if they will carry yours (and give an appropriate bulk discount or consignment deal).

- Write a guest article for their newsletters to gain exposure to new audiences. This can result in new speaking invitations.

#6-Newsletter Subscriptions

- At every event, provide a way for audience members to sign up to receive your newsletter. A growing mailing list is an invaluable marketing tool. It's one more way word of mouth can help you get more speaking opportunities.

- Your newsletter can be in paper or e-blast format.

- Offer incentives to sign up for your newsletter, such as a free downloadable PDF, mp3, or video clip. (Follow current regulations for capturing their e-mail address.)

- Make sure your e-newsletters are sharable by providing share buttons for e-mail and social media accounts. Most e-blast servers have this capability built in to their templates.

#7-Increase Website Traffic

- Find new places to post Web address links, such as guest blogger posts, bios, social media, mailers, etc. One place we often overlook is our e-mail signature line. Your e-mail server probably has a signature program that allows you to set this up with font style and color to fit your branding. This is the place to mention your ministry name, your tagline, your social media contacts, and your website address.

- Frequently provide fresh material on your website, rather than it being a stagnant page. If there's no new activity, it's no better than a billboard for marketing purposes. If your site is refreshed, it will increase visibility on search engine sites such as Google. One way your website will automatically be updated is if you load a widget for your social media feed.

Be intentional to increase your exposure in order to maximize your opportunities for speaking invitations. Rather than getting bogged down with a demanding marketing plan, focus on a strategic, step-by-step agenda. Instead of being overwhelmed trying to promote yourself, you'll be excited by the everyday ways you can interact with your audience. You're seven steps away from new speaking opportunities.

SETTING UP YOUR PRODUCT TABLE

Most speakers increase their earnings by having products for sale. Some call these B.O.R. (Back Of Room) products. When addressing your audience, you might want to call it a resource table (my pick because I like offering resources that empower attendees). Or even the autograph table if you like. (That establishes you as an expert on the subject.)

Audiences are more likely to wait in line for your products if they relate to you. And they are more likely to relate to you if you've gotten acquainted during any of the non-speaking moments of the event. Sales actually start before the event begins, when you are mingling to greet attendees as they arrive. Make genuine conversation—don't merely "press the flesh" and "work them up" even though you might have been trained to do it that way. (It's also a lot easier to interact when you make it about them rather than about you.)

Why Have a Resource Table?

- Honorariums for speaking don't pay for the number of hours you've invested in the event (promo to find the event, studies to customize the talks, communication with the event planning team, travel time, time away from family, etc.). Selling products helps supplement your event income.

- Offering resources also sends additional materials home with the audience. There's nothing more disheartening at the end of your time with a group than feeling like you barely scratched the surface of the information you wanted them to have. Back-of-room products help you continue to make a difference in their lives well after they leave the event.

- Attendees inspired by your message want to buy your products right away—like an impulse purchase. They are less likely to buy your products online or at a store once they return home.

- Consider offering a discount bundle if they purchase three products. This is the most popular sales strategy of some of my colleagues.

How to Display Product

- Set up your table in a way that looks like a mini-bookstore. Bring everything you need to give this a professional touch: drapes, pictures, book stands. Be sure any cloth you bring is wrinkle-free (crushable) and travels well if you're flying or press it after you arrive.

- Create readable signage that fits the look of the table. The font needs to be large enough and clear enough to read at a glance. Use upright Lucite® sign holders for price lists, promo information, etc. Also have freebie literature in professional-looking holders (brochures, business cards, bookmarks, oversized postcards, rack cards, etc.)

- Add dimension to your display. Consider stacking to create height. Study tablescaping techniques used for dinner tables and banquet serving tables. Put books or boxes underneath the tablecloth to have a variety of heights. Stack the products to be pleasing to the eye.

- Use gift-packaging ideas. This decorates the table and gives the consumers ideas for their purchases.

- Locate the product table in high traffic areas—don't allow anyone to tuck you away in a remote corner.

- Be sure there is more than one time to visit the product table—people may come back later to get the books signed.

- You don't have to display your entire inventory on top of the table—set up enough so it is appealing to the eye and leave the rest under the table for easy restocking.

How to Sell Product

- Mention a product during your speech if it benefits the audience, not as a sales tactic. Better to undersell and over-deliver.

- Have the emcee mention it twice. Include product information in the written bio you give the emcee to use when introducing you to the group. And when the emcee comes up at the end of the program, have them briefly mention some of the products again (or a special event deal). This gives you time to get to the back of the room to prepare to interact with the audience.

- Link to a story. People prefer to hear product pitches in an organic way rather than sounding like an advertisement. When transitioning to a story, you can mention "In my book, (give the title), I share this story." But don't give them a tease that says they have to buy the book to hear how the story turns out. That is off-putting.

- Give away a freebie and have the recipient come to the stage to retrieve it (giving product visibility). Or pick someone in the back of the room to win and have someone walk the product back to them, so everyone who looks back to see the book delivered also sees the resource table ready for them at the end of the session. This helps glue the impression in their minds so they remember to stop by your table.

- Have a volunteer assist you with the book table so you can spend more time with each person who stands in line to speak to you about their aha! moment from the program and to sign their books.

- Have a fishbowl for names—encourage attendees to drop their business cards or names in the bowl to sign up for your newsletter and also be entered in a giveaway. This gives them incentive to visit your table. In your next newsletter, thank those who attended that specific event.

Kinds of Products

- Stock the most obvious product—books you've written.

- Sell product tie-ins. For each book on your table, pull out a theme and come up with gifts that fit with that topic. Or if you're selling teaching CDs on specific topics, tie in some products that fit with the subject matter. It helps imbed the keywords of your business/ministry in their minds, and it helps you sell more product. Remember not everyone reads books, but most people like to take home a memento from an event.

- Make workbooks to go along with your books, or if you aren't published yet, to go along with your speaking programs. These are like guided journals that ask interactive questions and provide material from your speeches as well as additional resources you couldn't fit into your talk.

- Offer books on your topics/niche written by others. If you refer to others in your speech, work out a deal to sell their books at your table. The publisher or author will often give you a discounted price on books you purchase in bulk and will appreciate the cross-promotion.

- Give out purchase cards for how to buy your e-books online. Part of the product announcement can be to welcome the audience members to pull out their smart phones and order the e-book on the spot.

- Self-print books or booklets at your home office or by an office supply store. They can bind it, or you can use a comb-binding machine. Be sure this is quality if you do it. Better yet, use an online book publisher like KDP at Amazon for your self-publishing needs.

- Make custom jewelry that ties in with your core messages—such as reminder jewelry with single words. I hire someone to make these for me.

- Craft key-phrase cards. Pull out quotes and key phrases from your messages. These can be printed by you and laminated, or professionally crafted. Even business card paper will work in a pinch. I've seen some connected by a simple key ring, with the cards hole-punched. Others are put together in a sleeve or cute packaging container. Use your imagination. Look on Etsy and Pinterest for ideas. Shorter phrases and words can be made into magnets.

- Create audio CDs of your lectures or other motivational materials or music CDs if you sing. (This is another reason to record your events—if you are pleased with the results you can duplicate them for very little money and sell at future events.)

- Burn Document PDFs (so they are read-only format) onto CDs.

- Make sure you have products at a variety of price-points because some will not be prepared to buy at the event.

- Include some free items at the table and mention them during your promo time to help drive traffic to the table.

- Call some of your products sharables, such as an audio or video recording of that day's program. Consumers who heard it live may want to share it with others.

- Make a quality-packaged CD of a lecture, plus a quality-bound workbook or interactive guide to go with it. The retail price could be $15-$25 and you have approximately $5-$7 in cost.

Offer Purchase Incentives

- Buy one at full price, get one at a discount.

- Gift with purchase—add a small something for free that they can't get any other way (like a CD of a lecture or a magnet) when they purchase an item.

- Offer a today-only pack of items for a discounted price when purchased together.

- Bundle items and call it a fun package name. Such as a *Girlfriend's Time Out Kit.*

- Have gift bags that go with your themes. Bigger purchases get them free. This gives them an instant gift for someone or helps them carry their products home without fumbling.

- Include something for children. Moms often tell the kids before they leave home for the event, "I'll bring something home for you."

- Put a coupon in the event bag or folder attendees get at the beginning of the event that gives added incentive for them to visit the book table. Have copies of the coupon on signs and posted in various places saying, "Don't forget to redeem your coupon."

- Offer more coupon incentives at the table for attendees to use once they get home. For example, provide a free downloadable when they sign up for your newsletter or blog.

Coupons could offer special deals for teleconference calls, life coaching, e-books, mp3 recordings, podcasts, etc.

- Give a speaking demo CD and speaker packet to every event planner and ministry director in attendance. What little expense you are out can easily be recouped with new bookings.

Other Issues

- Look into the fees to ship your products to the event if you fly. Also weigh out the cost of licensing, permits, and taxes for each state.

- Consider asking a local bookstore to sponsor your product table. (Request the products you want them to supply. They deal with the inventory and labor, and you get the royalties without the hassle of shipping product or dealing with sales tax or permits.)

- Work out legal consent if your host is recording the event so it doesn't create competition for your sales table.

- Bring a cash box or pouch, a way to process credit card purchases (such as a mobile device app), pens, and gifts for volunteers.

- Provide a way for audience members to place orders. You can also take pre-orders this way for products that aren't released yet.

- Consider donating part of the proceeds to a local charity and mention that during your program. Or donate it to a national charity that ties in to your cause or to the theme of the event.

Problems to Prevent

How to estimate the amount of products to bring? This is a difficult question because often the smaller venues sell more products per person than the bigger venues. We assume this is because the smaller venues don't have the exposure to some of these great products as bigger venues. Also it's probable they have fewer quality speakers hosted in their venue and are more likely to feel blessed to have such a high caliber speaker. Since it's a bigger deal to them, they want to take a reminder of the special event home with them.

When you are standing at the back-of-room table, don't allow one person to monopolize your time. Rehearse ways to end the conversation with someone who doesn't get subtle hints. It's not fair to the ones who have waited to talk to you if someone ahead of them takes more than the appropriate amount of time. And if you are offering autographs, you need to be able to stay up with the pace of the book sales. (I discuss cling-ons in another section.)

Be sure everyone is familiar with your products ahead of time. This prepares the volunteers in advance to help sell your resources, and it helps the event promoters advertise your products prior to the event so audience members come prepared to buy. One way to communicate this information is to have a product sheet in the information kit you have sent to the event planner. List your inventory with descriptive blurbs if necessary. This helps them have the appropriate table set up for you and it helps inform everyone what you will have available.

Sending a photo of how your product table looks will help them fit it into the décor. And this is a good time to mention to the set-up team that the table needs to be in a high-traffic area. If you have it all spelled out in the product sheet, you won't have to say it verbally and won't come across as a diva who questions their competency.

If you don't have books published yet, brainstorm ideas for products related to your programs and messages. Plan ways to stock resources to sell at events.

☙

Offering a resource table at your events allows you to earn more income while also extending your ministry to attendees once they go home. If it's well worth doing, it's worth doing well.

WORKING FROM HOME

Working America is working more and more from home. During this section, I discuss how to overcome the challenges and maximize the benefits of this arrangement. Setting up a professional home office will help you succeed at your speaking goals. When you treat your speaking ministry like a job, you will see it flourish.

Challenges of Working from Home

- It is difficult to separate personal and professional lives.

- There are lots of distractions from the television, e-mail, etc. You also deal with interruptions from others, family, and even pets.

- People don't take your work as seriously when you don't go out to an office. They treat it like you are enjoying a hobby rather than working a career.

- It's hard to relax when you see your work "mocking you" as you try to take a break or some days off.

- You're at greater risk of burnout by not shutting down and shutting off.

- You must be a multi-tasker because you will juggle home chores and work projects at the same time.

Your Workspace

Set up a functional workspace that works for your personality. Have a good chair. Mesh-backed or comfy leather perhaps. It's worth spending money on. Decide on the best office equipment to suit your needs. Some of my favorite things:

- Professional quality laser printer (not a home quality ink jet printer)
- Assortment of high-quality paper—not cheap copy paper
- Multi-function copier, printer, fax machine
- Postal service scale and postage printer
- Filing system
- Desk
- Credenza
- Wi-Fi
- Organizers (and more organizers)
- Phone system with headset for hands-free calls
- Bookcases for books and collectibles for the personal touch

Create an environment that best brings you to a productive frame of mind. Some need music, some need the white noise of TV, some need quiet. Some respond to the stimulation of bright colors, while others require subtle hues. You might be more creative when all your senses are challenged (like burning a candle, drinking a tasty beverage, adjusting the lighting and room temperature, being comfortable, etc.). Figure out what works for you.

Your Schedule

Start the day properly. Have a good breakfast, spend some time alone to sit and do whatever. Relax, let your mind wander. Pray. Dispel the *I hate working* frame of mind. If you start your work hours grumpy and dreading your projects, you're setting yourself up for failure.

Establish your work schedule so you do fewer demanding jobs during your less productive hours and most demanding jobs when you are most productive. Are you a morning person? If so, put together your task-list the night before and hit the day running. Are you a night owl? If so, you might choose to work after the family is in bed at night. Of course, some of your work will require regular office hours if you need to make phone calls or interact with others.

Work with time slots if you need to compartmentalize your projects. This moves you quickly between tasks without needing to kick-start each time. Such as going from writing new speaking programs, to marketing, to creating a newsletter, to working on your calendar. Learn how to stop and start projects without carrying the thoughts of the old project into the time you need to work on the new project. This requires the ability to put on blinders to the other work still pending.

Your Breaks

Plan for breaks and meals. If you need to do a personal task during the workday, plan when you will make up that time at night or on the weekend. Explain to family and friends that if you take time off during your work time for a personal reason, you have to make it up because no one comes in to do your work while you do something else. Make sure others know the best time to call so they don't bother you during your work hours unless it's urgent. When you think of your work as requiring a certain number of hours or projects completed before you go to bed, you treat it like a real job.

On your scheduled breaks, do something that helps you vent frustrations, freshen your weary mind, and relax your body. You might find one of these works for you: playing electronic games, checking in on social media, taking a mini-walk, cooking a new recipe, running an errand, taking a power nap, or enjoying a hobby.

If you find yourself hitting the wall of non-productivity, work around the obstacle. You might try a break and see if one of the above activities helps you get back on track. Or work on a task that needs little focus for a while until your brain catches up. Don't allow procrastination to kill your progress.

Your Organization

Keep three lists of three. The first list has three things you will do today. The second is three things you'd like to get done but aren't essential. The third is three things that need to be done at some point. It doesn't seem nearly as overwhelming to tackle three things as it does to see nine tasks staring you in the face. This frees you up to focus on the work rather than feeling paralyzed by your to-do list.

Pay attention to your accounts so you know what income is coming in and what your projected income is for the next few months, broken down by the month. Know how much you need to bring in to pay the bills, and then set a second goal that is a bit more so you can get ahead. You are less inclined to procrastinate or fritter away your time if you realize this one fact: no worky, no money.

You're the Boss of You

Being able to motivate yourself is critical when you work at home. Be willing to own your mistakes and adjust when necessary to get back on track. "The buck stops here" applies to anyone who is self-employed—including speakers. Be hard on yourself, but not too hard!

If you employ others in any capacity, balance the desire to become the type of boss you always wish you had with the practicality of being the most efficient team. I've found it works best to evaluate your team players' giftedness and create a job description that fits their abilities and personalities.

Your Professional Reputation/Integrity

- Answer the phone as a business, especially during business hours. I answer, "This is Kathy" and that way it sounds professional, but not too stiff for friends.

- Answer your e-mails like a professional. If in doubt, sit on it overnight before you hit send.

- Don't get behind on e-mail correspondence, invoices, paying your bills, etc. It can snowball if you let it. This is another time when you need to put blinders on to the laundry piling up or dishes in the sink. Get your work done.

- Know tax laws and abide by them. Take every work-at-home tax break you can take. But don't hide income. We can't expect God to bless our businesses if we operate in darkness instead of Light.

- Make your business decisions based on your Christian worldview. Don't check your Bible at the door!

Create the right balance of personal and professional on your social media sites. Always assume someone who might hire you can read whatever you put there—and see the photos. What would be fine for a few friends to joke about isn't the professional impression you want to leave. I don't depend on my privacy settings to hide what I want to keep personal—I assume everything is open to the public.

Thankfully I've had good experience in this fishbowl setting, since I was a pastor's wife for over thirty years. Also assume others will deem you guilty by association if someone else posts something questionable on your page. The best policy is to delete anything that isn't appropriate, and let your friend know you have to limit what is posted due to being in the public eye. Untag yourself on photos that put you in a negative light. (And of course my first rule of thumb is that as Christian communicators, we want to avoid any questionable activity or conversation anyway.)

Hiring Staff

When I first started my communications business in 2001, I figured I'd be a freelancer, which sounded a lot like free spirit. For me, that worked well. I could juggle a busy ministry with my husband and also do my work. But it was part-time, and some days I treated it more like a hobby than a business. Then I got serious with it and dug in. Because of that, the work expanded, and I found myself working more hours than I could handle.

One way I managed my time was to reach out for help. I hired my first assistant. She worked solely on a contract basis, project by project. I learned her giftedness, and trained her in certain areas, and soon she started working for me on payroll, part-time.

I also hired a housecleaner for a half day a week. Then as business grew, I secured a booking agent for about 20 hours a month to contact media and event planners for me and my clients. And I also hired a mail clerk to get books and media kits packaged and mailed. She worked by the project rather than by the hour. I never set out to be a boss but God had other plans for this free-spirited freelancer.

I believe God exploded the business at that point because I was willing to share the workload (and pay) with others rather than stockpiling the money. In fact, most months I paid my assistant more than myself, and figured it was my price to pay for being a start-up company. I'm glad I did because it gave us a great foundation to build a competent team to provide a variety of services for our clients.

9 Tips for Working with Staff:

1. Select staff with a similar passion and work ethic. Make sure their integrity and loyalty are reliable. I select workers who love Jesus, because if they have an intimate relationship with him, I can teach them the rest.

2. Assign tasks that match their giftedness. Sometimes I reassign roles based on strengths and weaknesses.

3. Communicate well and often with staff. This is especially necessary if you have a virtual assistant rather than someone working on location with you. Document through e-mail, work assignment lists, etc. so nothing falls between the cracks and no one gets ruffled feathers over misunderstandings.

4. Be sure to have face-time with your virtual assistant at least a couple of times a year so that you can rekindle a passion that creates enthusiasm for the job. There's something about spending time together that can't be duplicated online or on the phone.

5. Look into all the tax requirements of hiring staff. I hired someone to help me set up the withholdings for paychecks and for sending in quarterly taxes. Also look into worker's compensation and unemployment requirements.

6. Compliment your staff often. It's easy with the stresses of our work to assume our staff knows we appreciate them. Praise them often and share specific ways you like about how they do their jobs.

7. Evaluate staff routinely. Spell out what you want to see improved and provide the resources for that to happen.

8. Give bonuses or gifts for jobs well done. Restructure job descriptions or numbers of hours based on the evaluation and the workload.

9. Set goals. Ask staff what their goals are and how your company can help them achieve their goals. After praying and asking God to give you a vision for your company, set new goals for the future. Make sure your staff knows your goals so that everyone is working toward the same dreams.

Getting Help or Hiring Staff

If you have too few hours in your day to tackle your to-do list, you need help! If you want to rediscover having a life outside of work and contacts outside of networking for your job—you need help! If you're starting to resent how much you work compared to how much your mate works—you need help! Like hearing first responder sirens, help is on the way. First responders use a list of diagnostics to know how best to help their victim or patient.

Our List of Diagnostics

Determine how many hours a week you would like to recover. Perhaps you have something new you want to add to your life, but you can't do it until you kick something else off the to-do list. Or maybe extra work has been piled on you because a busy person can get things accomplished, but now you are burning the candle at both ends and running out of wax. An extra ten hours a week would make a difference between feeling your project list is going to make or break you.

Decide exactly what you do that can be delegated to someone else. Often, the first to-go items from your to-do list involve household chores. Cleaning, cooking, shopping, laundry, errands, childcare, lawncare, etc. Have a family meeting and decide if the chore roster can be divided up differently or if you should hire household help. Often, family members balk at pitching in to help until they hear how much money they can save by handling these tasks in-house.

Are there tasks for your job that can be handled by an assistant? Know exactly what they can do for you before you begin the hiring process. Will they be making phone calls, doing mailings, following up on e-mails? Make a list of what you can hand off to someone else and build a job description for your helper. Again, it's possible that someone in the family will want to kick in and help when they realize they can save the family budget a nice-sized dollar figure each month. But do not hire family if they aren't equipped for the task. It's a recipe for disaster to be the boss of a family member if their giftedness and interests don't match up to the project list.

Your Boundaries

Avoid volunteering for too many activities. Many people will assume they can request your help because you work at home. They ask you to run errands, pick up their children from school or be an emergency babysitter if their children are sick. While you may want to help your friends and family members, it is important to make it clear that your work is as important as theirs and that you have obligations to take care of each day.

Set up a system so that family knows not to interrupt when you're working. Some close the door to the office when they can't have distractions. One editor said he'd wear a ball cap if he couldn't be interrupted (his thinking cap) and if it was off, then that meant it was a good time to chat. I play a specific coffeehouse-style music station when I'm writing new speeches or manuscripts. When my family hears that station on, they know I'm knee-deep in thought and up to my elbows in words.

Keep your family informed of scheduled phone calls so they can plan their own noisemaking activities around your need for quiet. If that's not possible, take the call elsewhere. Sometimes I like to combine my daily walk with a long phone call if it doesn't require notetaking or facing the computer.

Turn off the telephone when you need to work without distraction. Turn off Messenger and e-mail notifications too. Shut off wi-fi unless you need it for studies. As I type this, I'm also wearing earbuds listening to background music to block out other distractions. (It also gives family members notice that I'm literally plugged in!)

Some need the discipline of wearing work attire and keeping standard office hours to be effective. I tend to do better when I'm not dressed to go out, because it keeps me hunkered down in the nitty-gritty of work. Each person is different in what motivates them to put on the mind of work. When I put make-up on in the middle of the week, my husband knows a video call is coming in or Facebook Live is about to happen.

Your Ideas

We creatives tend to get barraged with ideas while we're working on other projects. Keep a notepad and pencil nearby. Jot down work ideas as they storm your brain but wait to flesh them out until you have that project on your schedule. Keep a white board for visual reminders of your work so you don't get distracted. Create a file for someday projects. When your business needs a shot in the arm due to a slump, rejuvenate it with ideas from this file.

GOAL-SETTING GOD'S WAY

Two friends decided to go fishing. Bill had an odd fishing practice. When he caught a fish, he'd check it out. If it was really big, Bill tossed it back into the lake. All through the day, the same practice. Many hours passed until his friend couldn't take it anymore. "Bill, why are you throwing all the big fish back into the lake?"

Bill answered, "I only have a small frying pan to cook them up."

We say we're willing to pursue the dreams God has for us, but do we limit those dreams to fit into our lives' small frying pans, or are we willing to dream big? We can stretch our dreams to grow into God-sized dreams.

If we can do something in our own abilities and strength, then it doesn't take faith. And if we aren't operating in faith, are we living the life God has for us? Instead of doing what we know we can do, let's let God set our goals for us and be willing to step outside our comfort zones, and allow God to stretch us. Then and only then are we walking in faith. This is what it means to dream what God has for us to dream (instead of merely asking God to bless our smaller human-sized dreams).

God wants to bless you. He wants to give you the desires of your heart that align with his will. He wants you to succeed. Be sure to embrace God's definition of success, though, rather than a materialistic view of success. It's not about fame or income or status or belongings. Success is about being effective for the cause of Christ, using the abilities and giftedness God has uniquely assigned to each of us. When we strive for that kind of success, we will enjoy a deep fulfillment that all the stuff and friends in the world can't bring us.

Do you believe in your potential—the potential from God's giftedness in you? There's a part of you that believes it—that's why you're a speaker. But when doubts start to sneak up on you, remind yourself that you were created by God to influence others for his glory and for their good.

Everyone has dreams God has planted in them. Whether they are big or small, they have vast importance in our lives. But to turn dreams into goals, we have to wake up the procrastinator. With just a little bit of planning we can accomplish the goals God has for our lives.

Turning Dreams to Goals

- Ask God to show you what goals to set. Get specific by asking him to show you what you can do today to get one step, however small, closer to achieving your goals.

- Create a goal that's realistic but challenging—big enough to push and excite you.

- Divide bigger goals into smaller steps so you aren't overwhelmed.

- Plan ahead. Once you've broken down your goal into pieces, keep a record of it on your computer or in a journal. Give yourself deadlines for each step. Otherwise, procrastination might get the best of you. (And when others ask you to do something else, you can honestly tell them you can't because you are on deadline.)

- Brainstorm ideas. Wade through some silly ideas to mine the good nuggets.

- Be passionate. Striving toward a goal without passion is like a fire running out of fuel. Get excited! You'll only go the distance if you love what you're doing.

- Revisit and evaluate your goals and make adjustments accordingly.

- Consider new opportunities and options that come your way.

- Stay focused and believe in yourself even if others do not believe in you.

Set Your DREAM Goals

D: Does it make a DIFFERENCE in your community? (Impact and Significance)

R: Can you REACH it? (Attainable and Realistic)

E: Does it ENERGIZE you? (Passion and Giftedness)

A: Can you ANALYZE it? (Track Results)

M: Does it fit your MISSION? (Purpose and Calling)

Warnings

Things don't always work out as you had planned. Sometimes there will be resistance from the enemy when you pursue God's plan for your life. When you hit an obstacle, ask God to show you how to proceed. Sometimes he wants you to go around the wall, sometimes he wants you to tear it down, and sometimes he'll ask you to retreat and seek cover as he brings out reinforcements. Stick to your goals, but be flexible, based on his direction.

Don't share your goals with people who might wear you down. Doubters and naysayers like to rain on your parade. They are often insecure and jealous or feel guilty that they aren't allowing God to direct their lives. They don't like hearing how you are pursuing God's idea of success for your life.

Inspired to Dream

What would you attempt if you knew you could not fail? God wants his people to dream big so that he can use us in big ways to impact others for him. He uses public speakers to inspire and motivate audiences. It is all for his glory, not ours.

God wants to make sure that we dream big in his Word. The reason why so many people choose not to do this is because their dreams do not match up with God's Word.

Let's go catch some big fish and not worry about a frying pan big enough!

> *Now all glory to God, who is able, through his mighty power at work within us, to accomplish infinitely more than we might ask or think.* (Ephesians 3:20)

SECTION TWO

SPEAKING CRAFT
Working Up Your Program

ELEMENTS OF GOOD STYLE AND DELIVERY

Do you want to have a greater impact on listeners? Evaluate your speaking and delivery style. It's hard for speakers to know if they're hitting the mark—listeners don't provide a ten-point critique of what works and what doesn't. Be assured, you can improve your style. Delivering a speech takes skill and practice, with a focus on several basic elements.

Body Language

What does your body tell your audience as you give your speech? One way to hide your nerves is to recognize what your "tells" are when you're nervous, and work to overcome them. If you tug at your garments, look down at your feet a lot, scratch your skin, push your glasses up your nose multiple times, these are tells. Instead, you want to look comfortable—this puts your audience at ease. Their walls of reservation will come down and you'll connect.

Maintain good posture. You'll appear slimmer, more professional and confident. Good posture also opens up your lungs to take in more air.

Allow your entire body to give the speech, not merely your mouth. Use big and small arm gestures to tell a story, create a mood, or elicit a certain emotion from your audience. If possible, don't remain glued to your lectern. Walk to the side so listeners can be drawn in to your message. The pulpit acts as a wall sometimes—a barrier that keeps the audience from relating to your talk.

Eye contact is another important aspect of communicating with your entire body. If you look down at your notes too often, you will lose your audience. They want to connect with you. One way to work up the nerve to look into their eyes is to look slightly above their heads at various spots on the back and side walls. This will give the illusion that you are looking at them, without actually making eye contact.

I only recommend this for those who truly have stage fright. Truth be told, you're missing out on a blessing by not seeing their faces. They communicate nonverbal signals as to how they are receiving your presentation. You will see heads nodding (and yes, some nodding off). A few will appear to have comic book bubbles forming over their heads with lightbulbs brightly lit as they experience aha! moments. Many will encourage you to keep going with their smiles, their welcoming eyes, and their cheery dispositions. Why miss it for fear of a few stinkers along the way?

Passion

Do your messages portray your passions? Make sure your speech is written so that you can deliver it in a way that communicates your fervor for the topic. Include a real-life story to take it from the world of facts to the world of feelings. Engage both the minds and the hearts of your listeners.

Voice Quality

Do you use your voice to the best of its ability to communicate your message? Audiences have an easier time listening if the speaker has a pleasant-sounding voice—not one that grates on nerves. Use plenty of voice pitch, volume and inflection to offer variety, and the proper pacing to allow the listener to travel with you through the material.

You work so diligently to select each word to represent the truths you want to communicate, so be sure each word can be heard by practicing clear articulation, projection, and pronunciation. Prior generations took elocution classes to learn proper diction but we can rehearse to get similar results.

Notes

To avoid rabbit-tracking, have good notes. Decide if you work better with an outline, bullet points, or fully written paragraphs. I put my notes in a three-ring binder so I don't misplace some of the pages or watch them slide off the lip of the lectern. Others like a PowerPoint outline sheet or note cards. Some even use a teleprompter on their tablet. Experiment and choose a method that works for you. A few good speakers know their presentations well enough to go note-free, but most of us still do best with prompts to keep us on track.

PowerPoint and Handouts

PowerPoint slides can add an additional dimension to presentations. But sometimes technology has glitches. When that happens, be prepared with plan B. Make sure you aren't dependent on the slideshow to present your program. Have notes that work independent from visual cues.

Handouts also add an extra element. A note-sheet acts as a roadmap to help audiences follow along as you deliver the presentation. Some handouts leave space or underlines for the listeners to take notes or fill in the blanks. This kind of interactive lesson works well for certain venues—especially Bible studies, seminars and retreats.

Weak Spots

All speakers have their own weak spots. Evaluate if you tend to use filler words like "um" and "you know." Perhaps you've conquered those habits, but you have a tendency to overuse certain words. Record your work and critique it to identify and eradicate words that distract from your presentation. Make a list of your own weak spots and also be aware of trendy words that get overused.

Finding Friendly Faces

Mingle with attendees before your program. Get acquainted. This helps them feel like they know you. They'll enjoy the program more. During the program your nerves are diminished because you're not in front of complete strangers. Find a few friendly faces, especially if you are anxious.

In your mind's eye, divide the audience into sections. Turn your eyes to the first section and make contact with an individual you met prior to the program. Everyone in that section will feel like you are talking directly to them. Then move your eyes to the next section and repeat the same exercise. Do this until you have swept the room with your eyes while presenting your message. In this way, the entire audience will feel like you've had a conversation with each of them.

In all these techniques, be sure you remain authentic to your personality and message—don't assume the style of another popular speaker and think it will have the same effect for you. People look for realness, not an air that is unnatural. Work to polish your skills so they become a good fit and you'll find your audiences warming up to you. That's the best way to be assured they will also respond to your message.

Ending Well

There's nothing worse than ending a speech without an ending. It just sort of fizzles and sputters to a close. Other ending killers include:

- Repeating the same information several times to make sure they get it.

- Thanking the hosts, the listeners, your mother for bringing you into this world…

- Giving too much of a commercial about your product table.

- Stating this is your final thought and giving a point, then saying "finally," with an add-on point, and then with yet another point declaring, "And finally…" Saying you're going to end, and then not ending is like not landing a plane and circling around the airport again.

- Opening up for a question-and-answer session if you've already gone over on time, if the host hasn't requested it, or worse yet—if there are no questions asked.

It's quite possible the main thing listeners will remember about your message is your ending, so it's important to end well. When you craft a dynamic ending, don't sabotage it by tacking on anything after it. Make your concluding statement and then close your part of the program—let that last statement act as the final punctuation.

Why do speakers work so hard on their introductions but try to wing it when it comes to the closings? Audiences want indications you are coming to an end, like spotting landmarks as we get close to home after a long trip. When you do your part right, they will anticipate you are coming to the end.

Some potential endings:

1. A confession
2. A poignant heart-warming story
3. A challenge
4. A powerful quote
5. Lyrics to a song
6. Restating a key phrase (called a circle-back)

In the same way ending a song takes work to find the right combination of volume, pacing, and instrumentation—ending a speech is a combination of trial and error and good instincts. It's an art form.

Sometimes the best indicator of a powerful conclusion is when audiences erupt in applause. Other times the best response is you-could-hear-a-pin-drop silence.

Finish well like a gymnast who sticks the landing. If the judges evaluated your ending to grade the whole speech, what would your score be?

ELEMENTS OF A GOOD PRESENTATION

H ave you ever wondered how you could improve your actual speech material? Oftentimes, remembering good speech-building mechanics helps. There are two types of speech writers just like there are two main types of novelists.

Seat-of-the-pants speech writers construct a speech start to finish merely based on an idea of what they want to say and the desired takeaway points. Each section of the speech builds on the previous sections organically as the speech-writers think of new material. They plug in their research and build the rest of the speech material around it, including illustrations that come to mind as they write. Even as they are delivering the message, if new ideas pop into their minds, they spontaneously add it to their presentations as they go along.

On the other hand, planners write speeches by constructing a solid outline first and insert researched information into each segment of the message. They still might choose to add spontaneous material while delivering the speech, often led by God's Spirit. So it doesn't matter if you're a planner or a pantser, you can build a good speech, true to your personal style.

Research

Researching material as you write your speech has never been easier. One way is to post a question on social media that ties to your topic and request input. Why do this? Not only does it ensure your material will be relevant to others, it also gets them invested so they support and pray for you. They'll follow how you're doing and will want a report after the event to hear how it went. As you enter all of this on social media, you establish yourself more as a speaker and you increase your traffic.

Here are other common ways to research your material:

- **Prayer.** Ask God to give you wisdom as you compile information that fits with your talk.

- **Bible.** If you are going to deliver a faith-based message, be sure it's biblical and use appropriate Scripture.

- **Internet.** Use your favorite search engines to hunt down material that will provide seed-thoughts for your speech.

- **Books.** Even though we tend to run to the internet any time we need information, books contain rich nuggets.

- **Niches.** Interact with your target audience to make sure the material resonates with them. They can fill in the blanks for you and provide additional insights.

- **Experience.** Brainstorm for real-life stories that fit well with the presentation.

Introduction

Your introduction is the hook of the presentation. It piques interest, excites the audience, and motivates them to be engaged. Address a problem your audience wants solved. They will receive ideas to deal with their concerns. They will listen because they want to be empowered to overcome their issues. Don't clutter the introduction with preliminary announcements, thank-yous to hosts or commercials about products in the back of the room. Jump right into the meat of your message with a tasty appetizer. Captivate them and tell them what they're going to learn.

Ideas for Good Openings

- Ask a question.
- Explain a dilemma.
- Confess a goof-up or fault.
- Tell a riveting story.
- Sing a song.
- Read or tell a modernized revision (original to you) of an old standby story or Bible text.
- Give a shocking fact—but tell it more as a story than a statistic.
- Share an eye-opening quote.

Extra Sources

Facts add validity to your material, making you more of an expert as you deliver the information. It's not merely what you think but what the data proves. Be conservative with your statistics and liberal with your examples. People want stories more than dry information. But a few skillfully placed facts will go a long way to prove your points.

Along with facts, using a few quotes adds extra flavor to your talks. Attribute the source of the quote and make sure the selection is short, so it doesn't slow down the pace of your message. Survey contacts on social media and blogs. With their permission, use others' quotes as extra insight regarding your subject. This has been successful for me. When the quote is significant enough, it will punctuate your speech and make it very memorable.

Some speakers enjoy using readings or poems written by others. These can be effective, but might be predictable or even stale if the material has been recycled and forwarded through e-mail too many times. Despite that, sometimes it's just the right touch. Or you could write your own fictional story or poem to spice up your message. Referring to Scripture or quoting Bible verses can also add authority and inspiration to your message.

Illustrations from Real Life

Real-life illustrations put legs on a speech. There are two kinds. One is planned ahead of time. Mark your notes so you remember the key elements of the story you want to share. This is a great time to step away from the lectern and engage the audience without any barrier between you and your listeners. Use good storytelling techniques.

Sometimes, examples from your life come to you as you deliver your message. These impromptu fillers are often the parts of your program that will garner the most comments. It's always interesting to see how God works in you and through you to say exactly what will impact that specific audience. Custom-made just for them. After you share the story, don't forget to segue back to your point so it doesn't appear to be a rabbit track.

Humor

Humor is a fun way to engage the audience. Not only is it entertaining, but it also prepares hearts to hear the serious parts of the message. But there's nothing worse than a canned joke delivered by a dry speaker. The best kind of humor is spontaneous rather than planned. A skillful humor writer knows how to write comedy into the speech and deliver it with hilarious results. Use something funny if you're funny. If you're not, leave it for the experts and focus on your unique style of speaking.

Music

Another element of a good program requiring special talent is music. If you can sing or play an instrument, and it fits your presentation, it's a wonderful addition. Like humor, music can open ears and hearts for hearing the serious part of the message. It can set the mood of the event and allow the audience to get to know a different side of you. Be sure to let your event planner know you have songs prepared that go with the message and ask if they want you to include it. Some have selected other talent they plan to use. Other times, they will ask you for a song list that fits with your message, and their music team will use selections from that list.

By including the right elements in your program, you can offer a dynamic event that works best with your abilities and also fits that specific audience. The perfect combination for a successful program.

A SPEAKING CRITIQUE

No matter where you are in your speaking career, it's a good time to get a speaking critique. One way is to conduct a self-evaluation after your speeches. As scary as it might be for you, consider asking others to give you feedback. We are all blinded to the idiosyncrasies that detract from our speaking. Be open to their suggestions to improve our future talks.

Recruiting a Critiquer

There are several ways to recruit a critiquer to evaluate your speech as well as give feedback of you as the speaker. However you go about it, make sure you ask someone who can be objective. Some of our contacts are wired to be cheerleaders more than critiquers. Rah-rah types make for great morale boosters. But they are often to blame for average (or less-than-average) acts entering national talent contests. These singers and dancers believed the cheerleaders who told them how good they were. They weren't prepared for the negative comments by the judges. In a similar fashion, knowing that some of our loved ones might be blinded to our flaws, choose an unbiased individual who is knowledgeable about the mechanics and goals of public speaking.

Setting up a Critique

1. Plant friends or colleagues in the audience with critique forms. Ask them to give a fair evaluation. If they are also speakers, offer to do the same for them. Just like a writers' critique group, learn to be tactful in providing constructive criticism, and always point out the positive aspects as well as the issues that still need work.

2. Send out a video link to speaking peers, and barter critiques with each other.

3. Hire a speaking coach or trainer to evaluate you in-person or critique your video.

4. Join a speaking group like Toastmasters that offers peer critiques.

5. Attend a speaking conference that provides critiques as part of the services offered. You might find this nerve-wracking, but it's a great way to get professional feedback on your skills.

Elements in a Critique

It's helpful to have goals in mind for the critique. Write them ahead of time. If the critiquer doesn't have his or her own critique sheet, create one to use. Here are some of the elements I cover when I evaluate a speaker.

General Impressions:
- Overall selling points
- Overall takeaway
- Times when the audience seemed distracted or disinterested

Physical Mechanics and Delivery:
- Wardrobe and make-up
- Winning body language cues

- Distracting body language cues
- Effective use of the stage
- Eye contact
- Vocal quality, enunciation, pacing, pauses, and changes in volume
- Use of technology

Message:

- Effectiveness of the introduction (hook)
- Main points in the message
- Impact of the stories and examples
- Use of statistics and facts
- Controversial issues
- Filler words
- Off-topic adlibs or struggle to get back on track
- Misuse or overuse of certain words
- Appropriate and effective humor
- Statements that caused confusion or didn't land well
- Effectiveness of the closing. (Did it fizzle out?)

Feedback:

- Memorable statements and stories
- Specific suggestions
- Grade the speech
- Grade the speaker

Critique Examples

I asked my Facebook audience to share examples of times they received critiques for speeches, and how it transformed future talks. They were given input by: professional speaking coaches, speaking organizations, other speakers, event planners, audience members, and friends. Here are some suggestions they received in their critiques from others:

1. Don't save your most dramatic personal story until the last of four retreat presentations. Share sooner so retreat attendees

can relate to you earlier in the weekend.

2. Be intentional with eye contact. It's an emotional handshake to help with engagement. It also helps the speaker feel as if she's having a personal conversation with an individual in the audience. And then another person. And the next. This technique also helps with pacing, so thoughts and eye contact are kept together and one doesn't get ahead of the other. No matter the size of the audience, it feels more like one-on-one conversations. This will assuage nerves and radiate confidence.

3. Don't let your voice go up at the end of sentences. Many speakers do this, especially women, and it causes the audience to question the level of expertise and professionalism.

4. Slow down. When you talk fast your audience can't keep up. They can't hear as fast as you can talk.

5. Know your speech well enough so you don't use "um" every other sentence.

6. Don't trail off at the end of long sentences. When you use shorter sentences, you'll have more punch and impact.

7. Be aware of mannerisms that distract people away from the message.

8. Make sure your projected slide presentations are professional. Give only highlights on the slides rather than including text for everything you say.

Answer Their Questions

Make sure your speech answers these questions in a way that is evident to the listener:

- What is the speaker's overall objective? To educate, entertain, edify, empower or enlighten?

- Why is this speaker the right one to deliver this message? Something in the speech should clue in the listener to the relevance. Does the speaker seem to have either personal experience or expertise on the subject?

- Did the speaker come across as believable, passionate, enthusiastic, warm, and relatable?

- Is this the right speech for the right audience at the right time?

- Would the audience want to listen to this speaker again?

Don't let praise go to your head, or criticism go to your heart. It's difficult to hear feedback on your speaking, but it's a powerful tool to propel you to the next level of your career.

CREATING TURNKEY EVENTS

One of the ways you can increase the number of events on your speaking calendar is to offer full-service turnkey events. This means you provide an informational packet containing ideas to plan the entire occasion. Include enough components so the event planner can use the materials, whether it's a one-hour luncheon, a two-hour ladies night out, a two-day retreat, or a three-evening seminar. By making their event planning as convenient as possible, it gives you a leg up over speakers who provide a list of demands rather than a folder of helps.

You can create a physical or virtual event kit for the planners to use. To make economical packets, consider buying solid colored school folders on sale, and adhere your own logo or label to personalize it. Use glue dots to stick your business card on the inside flap. Burn documents on a CD to include in the kit. Or make an e-kit available with PDF and JPG downloadables. These materials are perfect for a planning team meeting, so they can envision the event easily and delegate the details necessary for a successful program.

Other benefits to the event planner who uses your turnkey event materials include: more registrations, less risk of a planning detail slipping through the cracks, a polished, put-together event to make a great impression on guests and regulars alike, and of course—fewer headaches!

Elements in Your Kit

Promotional Materials

- **Publicity kit.** Once you've secured the booking confirmation, provide the event planner with a media kit they can use to promote their event. Someone on their committee will be in charge of telling regional media of your arrival. They can help you arrange telephone interviews prior to the event to encourage their target audience to register or buy tickets, and also give you exposure. Provide a news release article that is ready to go (with fill-in-the-blanks for their personalization) for their local newspaper or newsletter. Also design a sample advertisement in case they want to buy ad space in their newspaper or freebie circular.

- **Interviews.** If they promote their event to media, it's like having your own publicist in their town. Be willing to arrive an extra day before the event (or stay after the event) so you can do more in-studio media interviews. Use this opportunity on their travel dime to connect with television and radio in their part of the country.

- **Posters.** Make these printable at different sizes and have a poster committee distribute them around town as well as place them at strategic locations at the church, business, or organization. Give them a tip sheet for placement, such as inside bathroom stall doors.

- **DVD.** Provide video clips of different lengths for the group to play in advance. This encourages registration and builds excitement. Depending on the size of the event, a video clip could even be suitable for a television commercial.

- **Mailers.** Design a mailer that can be printed and mailed or e-mailed using an e-blast server. Offer to distribute to their mailing list if they don't have their own server.

Print Materials

- **Bio.** Provide a printed copy of your bio, written in a format so the emcee can introduce you. Even if you sent a copy of your bio in advance, bring one with you. Several times an emcee admitted she forgot to print out my bio and said she'd have to wing it. Now I simply slip them an extra copy of my bio on the day of the event when I first meet them and mention it's just in case he or she needs it.

- **Handouts.** Provide duplicable masters suitable for interactive note taking. When you give attendees a handout with your bio and contact information on it, you are utilizing another free promotional tool. Word of mouth is a great way to get future bookings, and a no-brainer promotional freebie. Simple, yet speakers sometimes omit handouts if they are pressed for preparation time. Once you realize these sheets are like walking billboards, you'll see it as gold rather than paper! An informational resource is more likely to be saved and filed away than your speaker brochure because it is helpful to the recipient.

- **Program.** Give them a sample program for print. Even if they customize their own, this demo will cut their time in half.

Event Extras

- **Menu**. Make a list of foods that complement the event and provide recipes if you wish. You can offer three menus if you like: appetizers/finger foods, full meal, or dessert reception. This can be as simple or elaborate as they want.

- **Skit.** Write out a humorous or poignant skit for those groups who wish to use their drama team. It helps fill out your program and allows the group to have ownership in the event.

- **Music.** Create a song list that works well with your message. These can be led by a worship leader and sung by the entire group or used as special numbers by the music team. Also, be sure to note if you can provide music for the event—many planners love getting a "two-fer."

- **Decorations.** Many of the event planners I work with choose the theme for the event based on the decorating potential rather than selecting a message that makes a difference. You can show them how to do both. Include photos of decoration ideas, catalog items for favors, etc. Make a list of props they can borrow from around town to save money.

- **Games.** Games add an entertainment element to any event, and they bring down walls of the more guarded attendees so their hearts open up to the message. Mixers encourage the group to get to know each other better. Especially for retreats, games are an important part of the event kit.

- **Door prizes.** Provide a list of suggested door prizes that fit with the overall theme. These can be solicited ahead of time from local businesses, from within the organization, or written into the budget.

- **Facilitator helps.** Some programs call for breakout sessions or small groups. Provide discussion questions for the group facilitators so they are equipped to expand on the subject matter covered during the keynote.

- **Schedule.** If they've booked you for a retreat, seminar, or conference, they will be grateful for a suggested schedule. Once approved, it can become part of the printed program used to publicize the event. Explain to event planners that registrations increase when attendees are well informed rather than kept in the dark about event details. It also allows latecomers a plan for the best time to join the group in the middle of the program.

- **Checklist.** To ensure details don't slip through the cracks, provide an event planner checklist.

By providing these helpful resources for event planners, you lighten their load so they can concentrate on making sure every attendee is impacted by the occasion. You also increase your likelihood of being booked (and for a higher honorarium) when you offer a turnkey event.

SECTION THREE

SPEAKING CUSTOMIZED

Dreaming Up Your Niche

SO YOU WANT TO BE A RETREAT SPEAKER?

Have you been asked to speak for a retreat? There are special elements in preparing for extended events. When you are invited to speak at a retreat, don't merely consult your schedule. First, ask the Lord for discernment to accept or decline the booking. This is vital in any decision, but sometimes we get so caught up in wanting to make our goal for number of speaking events a year that we rush ahead of what God wants. He's the best event planner when both the host and the speaker follow his lead.

I cover how to go about getting bookings in a different section. So let's start with the steps that happen once the event is scheduled.

7 Key Preparation Points

#1-Select a theme. Some event planners like to request a specific theme to go along with their decorating or activity plans. Others ask to look at my list of frequently requested topics, so be sure to have a list available. Lately, my book projects also make good retreat themes. My most requested retreat is "Grin With Grace" to go along with my book and DVD of the same title. Often your theme will not only determine the content of your speaking sessions, but will tie in to the entire weekend.

#2-Set goals for the retreat. What does the event planner hope to accomplish during the retreat time? Knowing this in advance will help you customize an event for their group to get the best outcome. If it's a women's event, the goal is often to come apart for a time of spiritual refreshing. Other objectives might be group fellowship, personal spiritual inventory and intimacy with God, renewal, group unity. Marriage retreats provide helps for couples, as well as opportunities to rekindle their romance and commitment. Sometimes retreats plan segments of the event to minister to all aspects of a person's being: spiritual, physical, mental, emotional, and social.

#3-Keep in mind theological differences. You might be invited to provide a program to groups outside your denomination. Usually when you focus on the common aspects of our faith experience, you can't go wrong. But sometimes terminology has varied meanings in different denominational settings. Take time in advance to get familiar with the host's belief system and practices so you can keep the group unified with clear, uplifting, challenging messages.

I've heard many speakers say that as long as what they can and can't say isn't dictated, and they have liberty in sharing what they believe God has led them to present, then they have no problem speaking outside their denominational preference. Determine your own policies on where you will and will not speak, based on your theological beliefs.

#4-Ask if there are any retreat traditions. Attendees assume certain elements will remain the same in their retreat experiences from year to year. Asking about set traditions will help prevent unmet or unrealistic expectations. While discussing the retreat setting with the host, get a good feel of your surroundings in advance. Planning your program and wardrobe is a lot different for a hotel retreat with a spa theme compared to a ranch setting with a western theme.

#5-Determine details about speaking sessions. What speaking style will you use? Some of the common formats for retreats include: lecture, interactive, Bible study, object lesson, reflective, guided personal journaling, etc. It's wise to offer variety during your speaking to keep the audience interested and to achieve the goals set by the retreat leader.

Find out how many speaking sessions you will have, their length, and where they occur during the schedule. Learn if you are responsible for any other elements in the program. I'm often asked to bring the special and group music, the skits, the games, and even the door prizes. If there isn't a prayer leader, they may ask you to facilitate their group and individual prayer times.

Other special touches you might want to include in your retreat packet: printed handouts or retreat booklet, suggested decorations list, and craft ideas.

#6-Don't forget retreat etiquette. The key aspect of retreat etiquette is the simplest to state but the most difficult to heed—stay on schedule. Be conscientious of your time. Even if events prior to your sessions cause a delay in the program, do your best to get the retreat back on track. If the schedule is severely behind schedule, ask the event planner or emcee what time you should conclude your talk.

#7-Get to know the attendees. It's difficult for keynote speakers to get acquainted with attendees for the one or two hours you are there for a short event. But in a retreat environment, you have the time to connect—and it's vital to the outcome. When you call attendees by name it means so much to them. And when you show concern over the issues that matter to them they are touched. Come to the retreat fully prepared so you can use the extra time interacting with others rather than being holed up in your private room.

Don't assume you are only there to minister to them. It's quite possible God is going to do a work in your life as well. Be prepared to come away with a special touch from the Lord. You probably won't be as refreshed as the rest of the group, but you'll likely be just as revived. With the proper planning and preparation, you will be a blessing to others and will receive a blessing as well.

SO YOU WANT TO SPEAK FOR CIVIC GROUPS?

Often, we overlook the most obvious opportunity for speaking gigs—civic groups in our own towns. You won't get rich this way, but there are still many benefits to make it worthwhile. It takes just a little prep work to be ready. Check out these pointers, and you'll be well on your way.

Benefits of Speaking for Civic Groups

- Gain more speaking experience practicing your craft.
- Increase opportunities to book other speaking events from word of mouth.
- Sell books and products and expand platform (scope of reach) for selling future products.

Where to Look for Opportunities

- Service Organizations such as: Lion's Club, Rotary, Kiwanis
- PTA meetings
- Support Groups
- VFW and American Legion
- Hospital Auxiliary Groups

How to Prepare

Contact your local Chamber of Commerce or United Way to request a list of local organizations. Ask community volunteers for group contacts. Make a database of potential groups, the contact person for each group, the location and times they meet, and any other pertinent information. This will help you stay on top of booking details.

Learn about the organization so you can incorporate their values and mission into your presentation. Often you can do this by searching online or asking the leader for their membership literature. Study their calendar of events so you can personalize your talk for their group. Use the mealtime or pre-program meet-and-greet time to ask about recent projects.

Look over your existing talks and see if any can be adapted for general audiences. Most members are business people looking for ideas they can assimilate into their careers or their community involvement. They respond well to motivational and educational programs. Print your list of potential presentations from which program directors can select a program. Often you can design a signature talk that captures your passion in a way that is accessible to the general public.

Another approach is to think of a problem the attendees might have that you can offer helpful tips for solutions.

Plan Ahead

Provide your bio, written in third person, for the emcee or host to introduce you. If you give this to them in advance, bring another copy the day of the program. I've had several forget the bio at home and ask me to scribble down something for them to say right before time to start. The printed bio helps them not fumble and shows you are well-prepared. Keep it to an appropriate length, and if you know the one introducing you, give them permission to also speak off-the-cuff if they want to customize the introduction based on what they know of you. That always adds the personal touch.

Consider what you want the members to take with them. Often I have a small goody bag for each of them, with my business card and a few other items (office supplies, candies, etc.). Sometimes I make a survival kit to go with the theme of my talk, where each item symbolizes a point in my talk. Make sure you also have your promotional literature available for any wanting to recommend you for other speaking gigs. This is the perfect time to have a display with your one sheets, tri-fold brochures, rack cards, or whatever you have printed up.

Ask ahead of time if they will permit a product table if you are accustomed to having one at your speaking events. Often, they will agree to this since they rarely pay much of an honorarium. If you have an assistant manage your product table, ask your host if you can bring a guest with you. This ensures you'll recognize one face in the audience too.

Arrive early so you can become familiar with your venue. Pray the room—what I call it when I walk around to the empty chairs, podium and head table to pray for the members, the program, the leaders, even the wait-staff, to ask God to bless the time. This not only prepares the hearts and minds of others for what is ahead, it calms your heart and mind.

Greet people as they come in. Offer to help with any set-up going on so they view you as a worker-bee and not a diva-bee. Pre-program interaction helps them be more attentive and receptive when it's time to give your talk.

What to Expect

Civic groups need speakers for every gathering—often a weekly breakfast or lunch meeting, so they are accustomed to all kinds of presenters. Some are not professional speakers, and it shows. So they may have low expectations when it comes to their programs—and that's where you can come in and blow their socks off! This becomes a win/win because they get a polished presentation and you receive such positive responses in body language and feedback that you will walk away from the event with more spring to your step—ready to book a calendar full of events—big and small.

Be prepared for surprises. It will be more laid-back than a big annual event, and because of that, they might not stay on schedule.

Your twenty-minute talk might quickly get reduced to ten minutes because the emcee rabbit-tracked earlier in the program or they started late. You will have to think on your feet, but each challenge makes you a better speaker. Ask in advance what time your part needs to conclude and honor that, even if they don't hand the program to you according to schedule. Some might also want you to allow time for questions.

They usually do not pay you for your time, but they will pay for your meal. Some might give a small gift card. But what you gain in community networking makes it worth your while. Often someone in the group goes back to their church or business and suggests you as a speaker for a bigger event.

SO YOU WANT TO BE A MOTIVATIONAL SPEAKER?

Many events look for motivational speakers to fill their keynote spots. Consider what you are motivating your audience to think or do. The personality of a motivational speaker is usually warm, dynamic, charismatic (without being slick). If people say they are drawn to you and are inspired by your programs, you might make a good motivational speaker.

Evaluate what you have to say that is unique to your life experience. What story do you have to share that will provide special aha! moments to the audience? The best motivational speakers are transparent and authentic, sharing from their own lives rather than repeating canned material they've recycled from other speakers and writers. The keynoters who become high profile are those who have incredible stories of uncommon experiences. Do you have a story like that in your life? Are you brave enough to share it?

Take an Inventory of Your Life Stories:

- Have you experienced a unique second chance?
- Have you overcome a challenge?

- Have you found a way to not be a victim of your circumstances?
- Have you broken a cycle of abuse, poverty, or other dysfunction often passed down from family to family?
- Have you lived apart from your family for a reason or a season?
- Have you survived a traumatic experience or tragedy? A severe weather devastation?
- Have you left your old life for something new? Reinvented yourself despite trials and testing?
- Have you endured a shocking life lesson that can make a difference in the lives of the listeners by embedding a truth forever in their minds?

Who Is Your Audience?

Define to whom you are speaking. It might be:

- Nonprofit organizations
- Charity events
- Corporate events
- Civic groups
- Educational institutions
- Cruise ships
- Personal interest groups
- Parenting groups (at school, church, or community)
- Chamber of Commerce
- Common challenges/support groups (such as cancer support groups)

How does your message connect to the audience? Consider their needs and their aspirations so you can adjust your content to better fit what they need to hear. Also keep in mind the goals of the event planning team. They often are looking for a speaker who will help build morale as a group and as individuals.

What other methods from this book can you use to customize your program to fit the motivational niche? Perhaps you can use special visuals or music that will motivate the audience towards a more can-do attitude.

Be sure to add motivational speaker as a keyword when describing your services. Add it to the following:

- Your website keywords
- Your bio
- Your business cards and promotional print materials
- Your e-mail signature line
- Speakers agencies and bureau listings

One word of warning. Anyone can say they are a motivational speaker, so there is a lot of competition. Public speakers can easily put out a shingle and offer to motivate audiences. Be sure you really fit this category. Perhaps ask in your audience feedback surveys if they found you to be motivational. Once you've considered the other speakers in your field, define what makes you a better fit than the competition, and use that as part of your marketing focus. How do you plan to stand out from the crowd of motivational speakers in your specialty or region?

And don't forget the speech—is it specifically designed to be motivational? Or do you have an empty brand with no product to back it up? You can apply all the what to do and how to do it principles from this book, but if you don't have a good message, you will flop as a motivational speaker. Message is king.

SO YOU WANT TO BE A HUMOR SPEAKER?

Humor speakers are booked to entertain, but often the goal is to also provide other results. Through humor, a speaker can deliver great content in a format that is easier to digest. And event planners love booking humorists because funny makes money—they can sell more tickets if the keynoter is slated as comedic.

Humor

- Relaxes the audience and helps them warm up to you
- Brings people together (laughter is a common denominator)
- Lifts burdens, at least temporarily
- Breaks down walls so listeners are more receptive to your point of view
- Sneaks truths in along with the silly stuff
- Helps audiences remember the serious points better

Since humor improves our health and our perspective, and relieves the severity of whatever is bothering us, we can see why event planners want to book humor speakers. Audiences love to feel better.

There are many different kinds of humor. Some speakers are hilarious without even trying. They can deliver a serious speech but still have the audiences rolling in laughter (and the next minute crying buckets of tears). Other speakers are intentionally funny—and they've designed programs meant to produce laughter. They are original and fresh, so audiences respond well. But some speakers try too hard to get a laugh and their humor falls flat. Canned humor (think sixth grade joke books) rarely works.

If you are a writer, another way to know if you have what it takes to be a humor speaker is to see if you write it. If people tell you that your articles or books make them smile, then consider incorporating humor into your speaking as well.

You will know if you are meant to be a humor speaker because audience members will tell you how funny you are. The laughter is also a good indication. And if you notice spontaneous humor sneaking in to your programs unplanned, you are a born humor speaker. Not everyone can do this, like not everyone can sing. So be realistic when evaluating if you are a humor speaker.

I remember the first time I did something that resembled stand-up comedy. It was the opening session for a women's retreat. The ladies were tired from traveling. We needed a light start. Humor was the perfect avenue for delivering life-changing truths.

Once you determine if you have the raw talent, you can learn how to hone that ability to produce an even better program. Evaluate your favorite humor speakers. What makes them funny? What styles and techniques can you learn from them to make your own routine more effective?

Techniques

1. **Unrelated subjects.** Funny speakers often mention two unrelated things in the same sentence and then tie them together in a clever way.

2. **Puns.** Use puns in a fresh way. Like when the doctor told me he was going to get me plugged in with a doctor for a colonoscopy. I told him that was an unfortunate choice

of words. We both laughed, and it relieved the stress of a serious moment. Funny speeches can do that too.

3. **Exaggeration.** Use exaggeration in a fun way. Even Jesus used hyperbole to make a point. The more unlikely a point is, the funnier it is for the listener. Often with just a little doctoring you can take a true story and embellish it using extreme details to make it funny. The audience will realize you've left truth for fiction because of how unlikely the story becomes.

4. **Self-deprecation.** If you pick on anyone with your humor, pick on yourself. Magnify a flaw. Confess a fault. But make sure it's funny and not pathetic or abusive.

5. **Asides.** In the middle of a talk you can create a funny moment by stepping outside the perceived outline on a rabbit-track or confession or some other seemingly random (yet intentional) moment of humor. You can also talk to yourself as if the audience isn't in the room.

6. **Mystery humor.** For this to work it's essential that you don't let on that you're about to tell something funny. Avoid saying, "That reminds me of a funny story." When an unexpected moment of silliness shows up in the middle of a regular talk, it's more amusing than telling a canned joke. You tell a story that sounds plausible or inspirational, but then at the end of the story rather than wrapping it up with a predictable bow, take an odd turn with the closing and say something that surprises them.

7. **Life observations.** Another way to deliver fresh humor is to take a quirky or snarky look at a common everyday happening. To set up this kind of humor usually start with a question like, "Have you ever noticed . . . ?"

As you study clean comics to see what they do that works, you'll notice they often exaggerate certain body language and facial expressions. You can watch some of these routines on YouTube. Based on what you learn, make a list of what you want to work on, such as:

- Content
- Pacing and pauses
- Delivery
- Physical comedy (not merely body language, but stunts like Dick Van Dyke's pratfalls)
- Stage Persona
- Different accents and voices for different characters
- Make your branding fun too (photos, website, speech titles, newsletters, etc.)

Use some of your life experiences as topics for humor. Once you can laugh at something you've gone through, you're ready to share it with others. It has been said, "Humor is simply tragedy separated by time and space."

When I first discovered the internet, I used to forward funny e-mails to my mailing list (those poor folks!). I used humorous Top Ten Lists from the Web in my speaking programs. Then it dawned on me that everyone has access to these same tired pieces. From that comes a word of caution: don't use recycled humor. Instead, you can take something you find funny and use that as inspiration to write your own bit of humor that has similar pacing or scenario, but a new punch line. This brings grins rather than groans when you share it with your audiences. One way to experiment with humor is to post original one-liners on social media and gauge their responses.

Try out your humor on a variety of audiences. It doesn't matter if it's for an actual speaking program. When you're with a group in a casual setting or even one-on-one with someone, see what works and what doesn't. If spontaneous humor is the tip of the iceberg, then the base of the iceberg is work—humor takes a great deal of work that no one sees.

Don't use humor merely to get a laugh unless you're doing stand-up. Make your comedy relevant to your talk and you'll have one more technique as a great communicator.

SO YOU WANT TO BE A NICHE SPEAKER?

Niche speakers address specialty groups regarding specific topics—they aren't generalists. They have a narrow focus but possibly a large scope of reach, depending on how many people fall into that specific demographic. Specialty speakers can earn a good living, just like medical specialists can demand a higher fee than generalists.

Evaluate the unique features of your life experience to determine what you have to offer in the way of niche markets. Then do some research to add to the list of possible niches into which your material fits.

Reaching New Markets

One way to get fresh ideas for new markets is to visit online awareness calendars. Find an original way to tie your point of view to these awareness days/ weeks/ months. Add to your exposure as a niche specialist by writing articles to those target audiences.

I use BrownieLocks for my awareness day searches. They have a calendar online—each month has its own page. You have to scroll way down to get to the listings, but it's worth it when you see the variety.

www.brownielocks.com/month2.html

Example: Your niche specialty is chronic health issues. You can find some of the following awareness themes on the calendar:

- April: Informed Women Month
- September: Invisible Illness Week
- November: National Caregivers Month

Ways to Break Into Your Niche

1. Write online content.

2. Offer articles for an organization's newsletters, mailings, blogs, tutorials, and more.

3. Pitch speaking programs that relate to these special awareness themes, with the opportunity to have your resource table at the back of the room for book sales. Many civic organizations, charitable organizations, universities, adult education centers, and libraries are looking for unique angles to invite speakers to their groups. And businesses are looking for new ways to drive traffic to their stores.

Consider these specific venues:

- Adult education classes
- Conferences and conventions
- College events
- Corporate training programs
- Charitable organizations
- Cruise ships
- Government agencies
- Nonprofit organizations
- Schools
- Seminar companies
- Trade shows

- Mom groups, such as MOPS
- Support groups
- Senior centers

Keep the creativity flowing and you'll soon be speaking for new markets. This is a great way to open up new opportunities and also make your products available to new markets.

SO YOU WANT TO BE A FUNDRAISER KEYNOTER?

What sets a fundraiser speaker apart from other speakers? There's much they have in common with motivational and inspirational speakers, so be sure to read those sections as well. But a fundraiser keynoter tugs at not only heartstrings, but purse-strings and wallets.

You Might Be a Good Fundraiser Keynoter If:

- You have a powerful personal story.
- The audience feels they can relate to you.
- You can entertain with humor or storytelling.
- You can be a mood lifter and motivator.
- You can stimulate hearts of charity and volunteerism.
- Your messages help audiences realize their abilities and purpose in helping others.
- You can paint a picture for how their money will make a difference.
- You're not asking them to do something you haven't also done.

The fundraiser keynoter is a blend between inspirational speaker and persuasive speaker—you give an emotional appeal to help raise funds.

Your host will ask you to issue a call to action as part of your talk—often at the conclusion of your time. Usually the objective is an appeal to get people to act at that specific time to accomplish the goal of the event.

Some Appeals I've Seen Include:

- Asking them to make a pledge for a monthly contribution.

- Asking for a one-time donation for a specific cause within the organization.

- Asking them to make a call, text, social media post or e-mail with their smart phones to spread the word of their cause.

- Inviting them to the special booth to sign up for their mailing list.

- Presenting an oversized check for the organization's cause and then pleading with the audience to also contribute.

Being a fundraiser keynoter isn't for everyone—but it's a popular niche that needs to be filled annually for most organizations.

SO YOU WANT TO BE AN INSPIRATIONAL SPEAKER?

What's the difference between a motivational speaker and an inspirational speaker? Normally one is for corporate or civic groups and the other is Christian or faith-based.

You Might Be an Inspirational Speaker If . . .

- Your messages stir up positive emotions. (Do they feel excited, inspired, uplifted?)

- You tend to find the positive in a scenario or situation.

- You are adept at using Scriptures or quotes in your speaking material.

- You give pep talks to cheer people up and on.

- You live an inspired life. (You can't inspire others unless you yourself are inspired!)

- Your body language and tone of voice conveys enthusiasm.

- You use vivid word choices in communicating your presentation.

If you're an inspirational speaker, you'll be invited to keynote for a variety of denominations. Be aware of any differences your audience may have than your personal denominational choice so you do not offend, but also so you don't compromise your own beliefs. And if you speak for an interdenominational or nondenominational group, speak on commonalities rather than on what divides the group.

When you share something that captures your passion, you are ready to inspire others.

SO YOU WANT TO BE A STORYTELLER?

Stories do the important work of teaching life lessons without sermonizing. Even Jesus often chose the art of storytelling to teach important truths. Natural storytellers share vignettes that will entertain, hit home, teach, and be remembered for years. Even if the audience forgets your name, they won't forget a great story—if you tell it well.

Ingredients to Good Storytelling

1. Keep the content tight—don't belabor a point.

2. Use novel writing techniques to create your story. Include vital details regarding setting, characters, and descriptions. Employ all five senses if possible.

3. Craft each word to help the listener feel as if they are inserted into the story as a witness.

4. Make sure you don't rabbit track. Each sentence needs to build on the one before and be vital to the story or it only detracts.

5. Have a memorable wrap-up to the story.

If you're a storyteller, you will craft your presentation around the stories you want to share rather than plugging in stories as illustrations for your main points. Stories are effective in delivering incredible takeaway points.

I like using personal experience stories in my writings and speeches. The problem is, I'm such an open book that I forget that not everyone is comfortable if I tell the world about their part of my stories. They aren't ready for it to be put out for public consumption. I had to learn the hard way that even when I mention someone I love in a positive light, they might not like it. Sometimes it's wise to ask their consent. And if it's a story where they are put in a negative light, then don't even risk it—change the name and enough details so it will never make them look bad.

One problem storytellers have is knowing how much information is too much information. If you add too many facts, they clutter the story pertinent parts don't pack as much punch. You don't have to give a chronological account of every detail. Instead, give snapshots of important scenes in the story. When you add unimportant details, your riveting story becomes a bedtime story—never a good thing to lull your audience to sleep!

Don't put yourself on a pedestal as you share a story. When you put someone else in the spotlight, that goes over better. And when you confess a personal flaw or struggle, that's when the audience can most relate to you—not when you describe yourself as a perfect saint. So be transparent.

Communicate Truth

You don't have to tell them what you want them to learn from the story—let them have their own aha! moments. When you do that, you will be amazed at how God works. When you greet the audience one-on-one after you conclude the presentation, they will tell you what impacted them from the story, and it's rarely the same thing for everyone. Stories give your talks layers—audience members can peel back the layer they need for that moment.

How do you remember your stories? Good storytellers keep track. You might find some of your best stories from your social media updates, in your journals, or in e-mails you send out. Look around. A real-life nugget for a wonderful tale is always close by.

Audiences remember stories much easier than they recall facts. So use your story as a way to communicate truths and you'll see it make a difference in lives. Your stories will go home with them and before long, the ripple effect begins—it doesn't die with you.

THE WRITER AS SPEAKER

Even though this is a book for speakers, many of you are also writers. If you could choose just one, would you choose being a speaker or being a writer?

Perhaps your reply is, "Don't make me choose, Kathy! I couldn't possibly pick just one—I love them both!" That's how I felt when a mentor first asked me the question. So are you a writer who speaks, or a speaker who writes?

You Might Be a Writer Who Speaks, If . . .

- You write out your entire speech or message.
- You tend to be an introvert who speaks more due to passion of the topic than to the love of public speaking.
- You find yourself correcting the grammar of other public speakers (in the privacy of your own thoughts).
- You struggle with making your book table look clever and creative—you settle for orderly.
- You are most inspired to create stories and insights while writing, rather than in the middle of a speaking presentation.

173

You Might Be a Speaker Who Writes, If . . .

- You start with an outline or bullet points when you write, and then have to bulk it up to turn it into an article or book.

- You tend to be an extrovert who goes on withdrawal for human interaction when holed up writing for deadline.

- You find yourself evaluating the stage presence of other public speakers.

- You thrive on decorating your book table with a flourish.

- You improvise with ease during a presentation, inspired to share additional examples and stories on the fly.

And you might be so in love with words that you couldn't possibly choose one or the other. If you are a communicator who is involved in both speaking and writing, you may face some special opportunities and challenges.

Merchandise

Speaking events give writers an opportunity to sell their books or other products. With this comes a set of challenges, especially if the speaker has flown to the venue. How many books should you send or take to the event? Should you ship them ahead or pack them in your luggage? Will you earn enough in book sales to pay for the extra expense of not only getting them there, but also getting them home if they don't all sell?

Manuscripts

Whenever I get invited to speak, I first write up my program as fleshed out paragraphs. I save these to a computer file to later insert into book manuscripts. Then I go back to a copy of the speech and format it for speaking. I make bullet points and outlines instead of paragraphs. I save specific pull quotes to read or say word for word, to make punchy statements. I change the font from Times New Roman to Arial Rounded MT Bold. I change the margins from 1-inch to my preferred speaking margins. Top: .5", Left: 1.5" (to allow for hole-punching space), Right: .75", Bottom: 1.5" (I have vision problems with some podiums as I get to the bottom of the page, so I allow more white space there.)

More Books and More Speeches

Think of all the books you'd like to write in the next few years. Write up a paragraph summary for each book—an elevator pitch. Look over each one and consider how you can use these same ideas as speaking topics. Rework the paragraphs, keeping your speaking programs in mind. Redo your speaker promotional literature and online presence to include these possible presentations. When you are a writer who speaks, your speaking material becomes your writing inspiration and your writing material becomes your speaking inspiration. It's all interwoven. Why waste the brainstorming power for those blurbs? Use them for both!

Make Notes

If you find yourself coming up with new thoughts or stories during a speaking program, be sure to write these down after the event so you can use them in future writing projects. There's something special about the synergy that happens during a live audience to bring out new material. And you can tell if the new aha! lands well with the audience, like having your own in-person focus group. Don't waste that inspiration—use it. I keep a supply of all my speaking inspirations, typed up, in a file on my computer. It might find its way into an article assignment, a book chapter begging for an example, or an upcoming interview.

Consider transcribing the recording of your speaking event, so you can discover the nuances you added during the program that might not have been in your original speaking notes. This is another way you can make the most of your presentation.

As I heard a parent recently tell her child, "Use your words."

THE PREACHER AS SPEAKER

While I coached a client who is also a pastor, he made a smart observation. He said, "Public speaking is different than preaching. I want to learn those differences and become a better speaker."

Preachers are often invited to speak to civic groups and organizations. What do they need to learn to do this with distinction?

Others I talk to aren't pastors but sit under good (or not-so-good) preaching every week and that is their primary example of public speaking. They need to be aware of the differences between preaching and speaking so they can excel as speakers.

I researched this topic and found most articles wanted to draw a line in the sand and act like motivational/inspirational speakers shouldn't preach and preachers shouldn't present motivational/inspirational speeches and call them sermons. I don't think we have to categorize speaking like this. You can be a good preacher *and* a good speaker. What do you need to know to do this?

Consider Your Audience

Ask:

- What type of group invited me to speak?
- What is the demographic of the audience?

Don't assume your audience is just like the congregations where you preach. They might come from different walks of life and have different viewpoints. As a group they have experienced different speakers at prior events. Even audiences in other parts of the country have different expectations and unique "listening" body language unlike what you've experienced. Knowing your audience will go a long way in helping you prepare and present your program.

Consider Your Goals

Ask:

- What did the event planner book me to accomplish through my speech?
- What type of speech did they request? (Motivational, inspirational, fundraising, retreat, banquet, humorous, etc.)
- What takeaway or outcome is desired?

As a preacher, your goal is to expound on Scripture to exhort the congregation to make spiritual decisions that lead toward conforming to the image of Christ. As a speaker, your role is to provide a program that fits the goal of the host and the audience. Discussing this goal ahead of time will help you prepare the ideal presentation for their event.

Consider Your Experience

Ask:

- What real-life stories can I share to personalize the speech?
- What passions do I have that tie in with the group or speech I'm giving?

The best way to make your program different from their previous events is to make sure your heartbeat pulses through the words, and your speech isn't merely facts you've researched. Each presentation you deliver needs to have your fingerprint on it. It will match your brand while also fitting the request of the host.

Consider Your Gifts

Ask:

- What speaking gifts have others said shine through me?
- What public speaking skills have previously left me disappointed after I delivered a speech? What are my weaknesses?

God has gifted you with a one-of-a-kind speaking style. This is what makes your presentations special. Accent your gifts rather than trying to reinvent yourself. Don't try to copy others (although you can learn from them, certainly). Be uniquely you, while polishing the rough edges.

As you evaluate your weaknesses, decide how you're going to compensate or change to minimize these flaws. Don't apologize for them or spotlight them. Let them hang out in the wings while you allow your message to be center stage.

Don't Forget the Craft of Speaking

It's a joke among older pastors that a sermon structure includes an intro, three points, a poem, and an altar call. Today's sermons are evolving from that outdated template (although some pastors still follow that format and have powerful messages). The craft of public speaking has changed over the years, too.

The basics of speaking remain the same, though. Share from a sincere heart. Hook the audience with a riveting introduction and hold their interest with relevant or entertaining material. Challenge them without shaming them. Inspire lightbulb moments. Give them a takeaway that causes them to walk away with a lighter load, a renewed mindset, more information on a topic, or a passion to be a part of a project bigger than themselves.

New techniques often involve new technology. Determine what works for you. Will you use a teleprompter program on your iPad or rely on your handy-dandy 3-ring binder? Do you like sharing PowerPoint slides or providing handouts for interactive note-taking? Decide if you want to incorporate modern tools and resources into your presentation or if you are more the stand-behind-the-lectern speaker. You don't have to use all the newest resources to be effective, but you have to be effective if you use the newest resources.

More Alike than Different

I surveyed my Facebook friends on how preaching and public speaking is different. There are as many different views on that topic as there are styles of preaching or speaking! They agreed on one crucial element: the authority for preaching is the Bible, while the authority for non-sermons is either the speaker or the speaker's research.

What makes public speaking and preaching more alike than different? It's based on the one presenting the message. You are the common denominator. Whether you are preaching or speaking, make sure you share truth from a position of your own life experience. This will assure the audience hears a fresh perspective every single time. What do they get when they book you as their speaker? They get *you* dressed up in words. So don't leave *you* at home. Show up, shine out and speak on. The preacher as speaker—a very good thing.

SECTION FOUR

SPEAKING CHALLENGES
Smoothing Out Your Rough Spots

SPEAKING FOR CHICKENS

If we all gathered around a table at the restaurant, hungry for chicken, I doubt we'd order the same thing. The menu might offer chicken pot pie, chicken cordon bleu, chicken cacciatore, chicken fettuccini, chicken tetrazzini, and chicken parmesan. We'd all pick what's best for us, right?

Just like we wouldn't all order the same chicken dish, I can't give you merely one recipe for how not to be a chicken when it comes to public speaking. But I can suggest tips from which you can select ideas that fit you. Choose what works for you to not only survive the speaking experience, but also be successful in delivering the message to your audience.

Facebook Poll

In a recent survey, I polled a group regarding their public speaking fears and nightmares. Here's a list of what they shared:

What do you fear?

- Forgetting my words or what I want to fill in from my outline.

- Feeling like I have to look down to read my notes too much rather than looking out at the audience.
- Being the center of attention—in the spotlight. My comfort zone is behind the scenes.
- Not properly filling the time given—going too long or too short.
- Messing up the opening, which usually isn't written out in my notes.
- Being so nervous I can't read my notes—they become a blurred jumble.
- Losing my place in my notes.
- Nerves. The physical symptoms make it worse, like butterflies in my stomach, knees-a-knocking, heart palpitations, quivering hands and brain whirls.
- The unexpected. I'm not always good at quick recoveries when that happens while I'm speaking.
- My content won't be the right fit for the group. I don't want people to feel like I've wasted their time.
- Wondering if my message is what God wants me to say. I don't want it to be my agenda, but God's.
- Making a spectacle of myself.
- Rabbit-tracking—veering off from my notes and winging it (poorly).
- Everyone laughing at me.
- Being dull.
- Just bombing.

Why do you have these fears?

- I'm phobic of anything that takes me out of my comfortable introversion.
- I compare myself with others I deem more successful.
- I struggle with low self-esteem and confidence—too self-conscious.
- I'm paranoid. I fear everyone is judging me and waiting for me to slip up.

- I forget to breathe.
- I forget to refer to my notes and I get off track.

Remedies from survey group:

- I try to forget about me and think of the people I'm speaking to. It helps!
- When I'm passionate about the message and comfortable about my purpose in being a part of sharing that message, the nerves dissipate.
- I try to recognize when my fears are distorted. My fears and feelings often lie to me and derail me from accomplishing what God wants me to do.
- I practice enough that I know the words even if I can't read my notes or lose my place.

What Are You Afraid Of?

In order to combat your nerves, answer the what-if fears in advance. Look over the previous list of possible fears from our survey. Do you relate to any of them? Can you add more of your own? Take inventory of your fears. Then, beside each fear, come up with a remedy. Be prepared for any of your worst-case scenarios to happen. Then you won't be caught off-guard when they do. By facing your fears head on you can combat the butterflies.

Example Fear: I'm afraid the group won't like my message. It won't fit their needs or interests. It will bomb because I'm not in touch with what the group wants, or I'm boring.

Example Solution: I will recruit my prayer team to pray with me regarding this message. I will ask God to show me the material he wants me to cover. He won't fail me—he opened this door of opportunity for a reason. He will help me research the information that will work for this group. I will survey others to make sure I'm on target with my content.

I will remind myself that humans all have a great deal in common so if the material is of interest to me and to my test group, then it will probably be a good fit for the audience as well. And if I'm passionate about it, that zeal will ignite a good spirit in the room.

I won't bomb because I've bathed this event in prayer and so have others, and I've prepared enough to be familiar with the material. I'm switching my fear of the what-ifs to an excitement over wondering what God is going to do with this program. A new list of what-ifs that contains so many exciting possibilities!

How to Relax

Before the event, have a time of prayer prior to greeting others. If possible, pray the room. Walk around the room and pray for those who will be seated in those sections. Pray away the possible distractions (sound system demons, coughing, talking, other distracting sounds, dysfunctional heating or cooling, you name it). Surrender yourself fully to God's use and ask him to infuse your message. It doesn't matter if you're talking about a faith-based subject or a general speech—God loves to be reflected through you.

Practice deep breathing exercises—in through the nose, out through the mouth. Slow and deliberate. Do it correctly or you might hyperventilate. Cleansing breaths, not Lamaze technique! During the preliminary portion of the program continue preparing your heart and mind. Learn to be fully in the moment and at the same time discard any distracting thought or fear.

While the emcee is introducing you, utilize a combination of breath prayers and deep breathing. By breath prayers I mean short prayers that last as long as the inhale. Inhale a request, exhale a praise to God. Quickly segue from thinking about your part of the message to God's part of the message. Think of the takeaway for the audience. Get the focus off of you and onto the outcome. One way to shift from a self-focus is to pray for those who are praying for you.

Consider using progressive muscle relaxation. While you are seated prior to your part of the program, contract a specific muscle and then relax it. Don't forget to breathe while you do this. Start at the toes and work your way up to your neck. This stimulates circulation, relaxes muscles and nerve endings, and gets the oxygen-rich blood flowing to your brain. Now you are ready to mount the stage!

Nail Your Opening and Closing

Remember the audience has a lot on their minds, and your job is to get them to unplug from their reality so they focus on your message. Connect with your audience within the first few minutes. The same way an author must catch his reader's attention in the first five pages, a speaker has mere moments to draw in the listener. Allow each member of the audience to feel as if you are speaking only to him or her. Do this by walking to different spots on stage and by using fearless eye contact. Be authentic. Listeners can spot a fake.

Be Confident in Your Content

It's not just the spit and polish, it's the content, so make sure your speech has substance. Will it make a difference to the listener? What is the goal of the message? (Will it educate, empower, equip, inform, or inspire?) Real-life illustrations and stories will hit home better than a list of facts. When speaking of self, show your foibles and not only your successes. Come down off the pedestal of superiority and they will relate to you.

Tap in to Your Giftedness

Are you humorous? Weave humor into your speech, and don't be afraid to improvise if humorous thoughts and stories come up as you are speaking. Are you dramatic? Use it effectively in riveting storytelling. Sing? Add a song to bring home the point.

Show Your Heart

When you appeal to your listeners with your passion, they will forgive a few speaker mishaps and focus on your message. What gets you excited? Angry? Empathetic? When you are transparent with what I call heart-core passions, others will be glued to your message. They will forget technique and will focus on the intent. It's like a person who receives a poorly gift-wrapped package. They will excuse the exterior when they see the exquisite gift inside. Similarly, audiences will overlook any goof-ups when they connect with your heart.

Use Props

Listeners will absorb what you say better if you appeal to more than one sense. Give them something to see. Think of it as a grown-up version of Show and Tell. If you use audio-visuals, make sure they are properly set up and have a Plan B if there is a glitch. Often, using props works like crutches for speakers. It's like a singer in a competition feeling more comfortable when playing an instrument. It's not really hiding behind something; it's more like you have a security blanket with you that makes you feel more at ease. These same props work as object lessons, to help your audience pay attention and remember the key points. Make sure you don't use props to the point of distraction though—there is a point of overkill.

In the End

I don't think public speaking success has much to do with whether a person is introverted or extroverted. It is about the love of communicating truths and being excited about the message. It goes back to the song, "This little light of mine, I'm gonna let it shine." We have a lot of reasons to share with others. And at the core, that's what public speaking is. Sharing. Not lambasting people with words! When we realize that, we'll no longer quiver like a bowl of jelly at the thought of speaking in front of an audience.

6 TIPS TO SCARE OFF STAGE FRIGHT

A friend recently recruited my help so she could learn to be more confident as she prepared for an upcoming speaking opportunity at her church. Pam was scared speechless and asked for my tips. She wrote:

> Did you ever have a fear of being on stage? I always recall you as confident. Pastor asked me to read Scripture for a combined service of the Methodist and Presbyterian Church for Good Friday. I have never even made an announcement at our church. Bible study is easy as it is a small group and we are all sitting at the table. Any advice on stage fright?

I told Pam I could share plenty of suggestions but even though I coach others on speaking, sometimes I still struggle with a lack of confidence. Thankfully, there's a way to tap in to those nerves to bring added energy to your presentation. Fear doesn't have to keep you from serving. Here are more ideas I gave her:

Focus on others, not self, while waiting to go on. Praise God for the opportunity to read his Word. Focus on what the verses mean to you. Surround yourself with love and peace. Don't listen to an internal voice that makes you fear failure or pressure.

189

Make sure you wear comfortable clothing. Sometimes we wear something that's brand new. But it's not comfy and we start to fuss with it, making our nerves worse. When we tug at our garments, it also makes us look more nervous to others.

Rehearse ahead of time. Just enough to feel comfortable with the verses. Don't over-rehearse because that can increase your anxiety and cause you to stumble over familiar words.

Allow enough time after you get on stage to breathe before you speak. If there are stairs to climb up to the platform, plan ahead for that. Don't barely make it in time and then try to start reading or speaking right away. You'll sound breathless, because you are!

Don't feel self-conscious with whatever microphone they have set up. Just read out! It's the sound technician's job to make sure the audience can hear you, not yours. If you grab the mic to adjust it, or lean into the mic, it makes you look and feel more nervous.

Consider typing up the verses on a piece of paper in a bigger, easier to read font. Then you can always put that paper inside your Bible so it looks like you're reading from it, but you can see the words better.

More Tips for Speaking Scared

To add to the tips I gave Pam, here are some additional ideas to equip any speaker coming off the bench. A prepared speaker is equipped to deal with stage fright or stop it from ever happening.

1. Tell stories.

2. Have a strong start, a meaningful middle, and an encouraging ending.

3. Know your main points. These are your anchors and the takeaways for your audience.

4. Keep moving forward—don't camp out on any one point for too long. You'll risk losing the crowd.

5. Keep your eye on the clock. It's easy to lose track of time once you see all those eyes staring back at you. Honor whatever

timeframe you've been given by the host. You don't have to tell them everything you know!

6. Give them something of value. Keep your audience in mind. It's not about you.

Address Physical Issues

- **Dry mouth?** Sip water or have a mini mint lodged in the pocket of your cheek.

- **Knees shaking?** Don't lock your knees but stand with one foot slightly in front of the other.

- **Hands trembling?** Hold on to something—your notes, the podium, a microphone. Or simply put your hands together and squeeze. Imagine that squeeze being a vote of confidence from God.

- **Short of breath?** Slow down. Straighten up your posture. Take a deep breath.

- **Voice unsteady?** Think of your next point and say it with renewed enthusiasm. Remember why you're there.

- **Sweaty?** Prepare ahead of time with the appropriate antiperspirant or body powder. And don't sweat it if you still end up perspiring. No one will care—other than to empathize.

Consider the conversation Moses had with God about his fear of public speaking.

> *But Moses pleaded with the Lord, "O Lord, I'm not very good with words. I never have been, and I'm not now, even though you have spoken to me. I get tongue-tied, and my words get tangled." Then the Lord asked Moses, "Who makes a person's mouth? Who decides whether people speak or do not speak, hear or do not hear, see or do not see? Is it not I, the Lord? Now go! I will be with you as you speak, and I will instruct you in what to say."* (Exodus 4:10-12)

What if this had been you talking to God? Read what God told Moses. Would this motivate you to speak despite your fear, or would you ask God to send someone else?

WHAT'S HOLDING YOU BACK?

One of my favorite ministries is helping people identify what's holding them back from what God wants in their lives and helping them clear away the clutter so they can get back on track. I recently asked speakers what is restricting them from their optimal speaking career or ministry. Here are their answers, along with my input.

Comparisons with Other Speakers

You are right. You will never be the speaker they are. But they will never be the speaker you are, either. God has designed you with a unique purpose and style.

Feeling Alone

The enemy likes to make us feel isolated in our work and in our struggles. But we aren't alone. God's presence is with us and his people are here to encourage us. What is keeping you from reaching out to someone?

It's Too Big a Hurdle

Do what you can every day toward the goal, in small manageable tasks. Trade feeling overwhelmed for feeling satisfied in the accomplishment of doing the work. Your big idea will take time to materialize. Mountain climbers don't climb the big ones in a day. They pace the climb. Set up camp. Get nourishment and rest before tackling it again. One day they look out and they're at the top of the mountain! That's the same way we need to approach big goals.

Perfection Pressure

Will it make you feel any better to know audiences prefer flawed, transparent speakers rather than those who appear perfect yet shallow? They want to connect and relate to those on the platform. Speakers who strive for perfection tend to over-prepare and then sometimes have less than optimal results during the actual presentation. Motives determine outcome.

Not an Expert

Many speakers don't strive to attain bigger gigs because they don't believe they are qualified. Audiences aren't looking for boring experts who know a lot but tend to drone on. They are looking for a passionate, compelling story from the heart. This will educate as it inspires. Motivate as it moves. Look to be the presenter who speaks from the position of coming alongside rather than from a pedestal. You don't have to pretend to be something you're not. (And if you *are* an expert, be sure to humanize your messages to incorporate feelings with your facts.)

A Bad Review

Some speakers aren't doing more speaking because they've received bad reviews (or what they perceived to be negative but were actually neutral reviews). Sometimes the speakers didn't receive terrible feedback, they simply didn't receive any feedback at all. So, they assumed the event planner, host or audience member hated the presentation. We mortally wound our own speaking career when we assume facts not in evidence.

Working Another Job

Many speakers believe God wants them to have a speaking ministry/ career, but they also must work another job for a reliable paycheck and insurance. This leaves them with little time and energy to do the work of a speaker. If this is the case for you, establish a couple of ready-to-go programs, and let event planners know your availability.

Lack of Invitations

The number one reply to my survey was a variation of this struggle. Some said they lacked contacts. Others complained that they lacked opportunities. And some are waiting to get invited. What would you tell these speakers? Is there something in your advice you can apply to your own speaking life? For event planners to know what you have to offer, they need to know what you have to offer!

Distractions

A person who is full of life makes a great speaker. They are busy about the business of living life to the fullest. Their zeal is contagious. But it also causes speakers to have too many projects going on at once. The best way to handle this is to quit multi-tasking, and start compartmentalizing projects. Give each task your complete attention while you're working on it, and then shut it out when necessary, to work on the next project.

Shyness

I appreciated the honesty of speakers who admit they are introverted and find it draining to speak, yet they know God wants them to. Their shyness holds them back. What can they do? I've found when presenters speak on what I call "heartbeat" topics, they come alive. Their passion fuels them and they light up on stage. As soon as they leave the platform, they revert back to timidity. There's nothing wrong with that. Be the *you* God has designed you to be. He doesn't only lead extroverts to be speakers. He wants to use you. You will reach people with your quiet spirit that an extrovert will never reach. Just "do you."

Lack of Health/Stamina

Many of us struggle with medical issues that limit what we can do with our speaking business. We make plans, but then our conditions derail us. Don't quit because of your illness. Your lack of health hasn't taken God by surprise. He plans to use it, and everything else he has allowed in your life, to equip you to make even more impact as a speaker. Let go of your personal agenda for speaking and ask God to take charge of your schedule. Only he knows what is up ahead for your health.

The Single Biggest Deterrent

Self. You hold yourself back by accepting self-limiting beliefs as if they are truth. You've gotten so good at creating excuses that you've forgotten how rewarding it is to work toward the goals God has placed in your heart. You've taken the easy way out by blaming it on the Boogie Man. Don't let yourself off the hook. Turn your challenges into victories. Not sure about it? You succeed when you get in the game. You'll either win or you'll learn. But when you're on the sidelines, you only watch others living out your dreams.

ROADBLOCKS TO SUCCESS

Do you find you're coming up short of accomplishing your speaking-related goals? Here are some ways speakers are hindered in making progress. Can you relate? This could be why you aren't achieving your desired speaker outcomes. After you evaluate the cause, consider some of the remedies so you can change the way you're running your speaking business/ministry.

Too many commitments taking you away from speaking.

- What can you remove so you have space in your schedule to work more on your speaking business?
- What can you delegate so you have new hours to work toward your goals?
- Is it possible you got ahead of God when you said "yes" to any commitments causing you to feel buried in obligations?

Too many distractions during the time you've set aside to work.

- What interruption is more important than finishing your work tasks for the day? Sometimes, something that seems urgent isn't *really* an emergency.

- Determine ahead of time what you will do if you're interrupted.
- Figure out how to limit distractions and train your mind that this is your time to work.

Not setting aside specific work time—waiting to "feel like it."

- Doing any sort of work, whether for your speaking business, writing, or anything else, can't be accomplished on a whim. Yes, you might get some things done on your list, but surely not all of them.
- Don't leave the outcome of your goals up to your feelings instead of hard work.
- Decide if this speaking task is important, and how you will do it even when you don't feel like it.

In love with the idea of being a speaker more than actually doing the work of being a speaker.

- If you feel drained when you try to plan, rather than energized, you might not be determined enough to be a speaker.
- If your idea of being a speaker involves being in the spotlight more than making a difference in the lives of others, you might not have what it takes to do the work of being a speaker.
- Ask God if you're really supposed to be a speaker. A speaker has to work the business side of it and not simply enjoy the afterglow of having spoken after the event is over.

Doubt in your ability.

- God doesn't lead you to do something he hasn't equipped you to do.
- Pursue learning more about the "how."
- Get professional feedback about your speaking. You can go to a conference that trains speakers or join a group like Toastmasters.

Fear of the outcome when promoting yourself as a speaker.

- You don't know the outcome until you get the word out and see how others respond.
- You aren't in control of the outcome, but you are in control of how many event planners hear about your work. And don't simply send a mailer and wait for them to call you. Working for bookings usually requires follow up.
- If fear in possible rejection or failure keeps you from doing the work, who wins?

Lack of instruction in the actual craft of speaking.

- Seek formal training either online or at conferences.
- Read books and articles on public speaking.
- Speak in front of an audience. Then do it again. And again. (That whole "rinse and repeat" concept.) The more you speak, the more you learn to speak well.

Lack of encouragement—feels like you're doing it alone.

- Get involved in a group of speakers who will "get it" when you reach out to them for encouragement because of the trials that come with being a speaker.
- Create a team who will support you, cheer you on, pray for your requests. I call this group my wisdom team. They keep me lifted up in prayer and also give me wise feedback on any challenges or dilemmas I face. I'm blessed to have their accountability.

Not enough specifics in the goals you've set as a speaker.

- If you find it hard to organize the tasks needed to move closer to your goals, devote some time to brainstorm and plan.
- Try reverse storyboard techniques to craft the plan. Think of what you want the end results to be—the outcome of your speaking business/ministry. List each one. Then go

backwards to discover what you have to do in order to have the desired results. This will give you your action plan.

- Research what needs done to work your action plan. Create a file of these ideas, so when it's time to work on your speaking business, you know right where you left off.

Haven't really received direction from God.

If you don't know what he wants you to speak on or who your audience is even supposed to be:

- Pray.
- Read Scripture.
- Listen to God's wisdom in sermons, books and from others.
- Ask God to show you.
- Just like missionaries get a burden for the people group they are called to, ask God to give you a burden—a burning passion—for the work he has for you to do. This will fuel you. This is your mission!
- Don't move forward until this is firmly in place.

Often, we set lofty goals, but we don't evaluate why we're taking so long to get to the desired outcome. By evaluating what is slowing you down, you can actively work on a remedy so you can once again move toward the goals God has given you. There are other reasons besides these ten, so be sure to ask God and your support team to help you figure out what your detractors are. You'll get there. Keep your eye on the goal!

HAVE PROGRAM, WILL TRAVEL

Which is worse, over-packing for your trip and being encumbered by the hassle of handling your own baggage (not to mention baggage fees) or under-packing and missing an essential item? This section will help you pack just right for your next event, and also travel in such a way that you stay fresh for your first meet-and-greet at the baggage claim.

Don't Leave Home Without Them

- **Medical items.** Remember to bring all of your prescriptions and OTC medications on the plane with you—even the ones you seldom need. If an emergency is going to happen, it will probably happen when you're away from home. Airport security requires you keep prescriptions in original containers, not in pill organizers. Don't pack them in your checked baggage because you'll be in trouble if the bags don't make it to your destination. Also bring along a printed sheet of your medical information.

Be sure to list: medications, diagnoses, doctors (with contact information), surgeries and hospitalizations, medication allergies, and other pertinent medical history. When I had an ankle injury at an event and landed in the ER (and subsequently at a surgeon), this medical file came in handy.

- **Travel page.** Create a list of all the important contacts at your destination as well as at home—names, their relation to you, and phone numbers. Add the address and phone number of all lodging on your trip. Include your itinerary. Save this to your phone and print a copy for your travel folder. E-mail a copy to your family and to your hosts.

- **Hanging organizer.** Store your make-up, bath products, shaving kit and jewelry in one organizer that folds for travel. Include a miniature mending kit and eyeglass repair kit. Pack a body spray to use for your scent (light enough to avoid triggering allergies in others). Body sprays can also serve as a restroom air freshener. Keep this organizer stocked for travel so there are no last-minute packing fiascos.

- **Storage bags.** Pack clothing in special resealable travel bags. Compress to squeeze out all the air, and you'll get almost double the clothing in your luggage (and fewer wrinkles). Leave that extra suitcase at home. Be sure not to go over weight limit.

- **Spray bottle.** Bring an empty spray bottle and fill with water as soon as you arrive at your lodging. Hang up two days of clothing and spritz with water. Most wrinkles will fall out overnight. Stay two days ahead to allow for drying time and to give variety to your wardrobe choices. By planning ahead, you'll feel less stressed when getting ready for events.

- **Clothing.** Plan your speaking wardrobe so it's mix-and-match with clothing, jewelry and shoes. Sort of like grown-up Garanimals®. With layering and the right colors, it can work for most seasons. Only pack one extra outfit rather than your entire closet.

- **Program materials.** Take a hard copy of your speaking notes. Burn your program materials to a CD or save to a memory stick. Don't forget any PowerPoint presentations, song lyrics, accompaniment tracks, handouts, etc. Add a zipper pouch to carry receipts and CDs, and it doubles as a money holder when selling product.

- **Declutter handbag.** You never know when security will search your bag, so have it ready for extra eyes to nose around. One time, in a hurry, I forgot to clean out my purse before a trip. Homeland Security red-flagged me, finding a butter knife from a recent potluck dinner. They did a more thorough search and found my police-issue pepper spray. Fortunately, when I explained that it was Homeland Security who gave me the spray after special training, we all had a good chuckle. After the background search showed I had FBI clearance, I went on my way—minus the butter knife and pepper spray, of course.

- **Checklist.** Create a travel list to check off while you pack. You'll need a departure checklist, and another to use at your destination, when packing for home. You'd be surprised what you might forget if left to your own memory. My editor said she once forgot her Bible and had to use the hotel's Gideon Bible at the event.

At the Airport
- Call the airline directly instead of standing in line for a ticket agent, if you've missed your flight or connection.

- Keep track of your phone. My friend left hers on a windowsill at the airport and was quite relieved when they finally found it.

- Don't misplace your purse. It is easy to do if you also have a carryon. The carryon strap feels like a purse, so you think you have it, when you don't. Put your purse inside your carryon or wear a lanyard wallet instead of using a handbag. If you need a purse at your destination, pack it in your luggage. I have a laptop bag that I multi-purpose as a handbag.

- Be prepared for the security gate. Have boarding pass and ID in a lanyard around your neck (or use a phone app for boarding pass). Include enough cash for your day's needs, and a credit card.

- Be ready to remove laptop and shoes when you get close to the security gate. Wear easy slip-off shoes with socks so you don't walk barefoot (and prevent blisters).

- Don't forget to empty your water bottle before security or it will slow down your screening.

- Don't wear glycerin-based bath products (like lotion). Glycerin is from the same chemical as explosives and can set off security. If they wipe down the handle of your bag and test the cotton pad—it can detect the glycerin from your lotion where you gripped the bag.

- Consider subscribing to TSA pre-check to circumvent many of the security gate requirements.

With these tips, you'll be prepared for travel. And with the lighter load, you'll arrive at your destination less flustered—fresh and ready to go.

DEALING WITH UNEXPECTED CHALLENGES

When I used to promote a Christian singer/speaker, one of our favorite pastimes was sharing on-the-road war stories with each other. While you're in the middle of the situation it's not so fun, but after the event is over, recalling the goof-ups provides lots of laughs. Ever wonder why speakers start using a rider form with booking requirements? It's because a speaker has been burned and has learned to ask for what he or she needs up front rather than assuming every event planner knows better.

Here are a few of the stories I've collected over the years. First grin (or in some instances, groan). And then—read them a second time and come up with your own prevention plan so they don't happen to you. Or—if they do, be prepared with Plan B.

Housing

Have you ever had to share a bunk bed outfitted with rubber sheets because your bunkmate was still a bed-wetter? Or been escorted to your sleeping quarters—in the sleeper of a semi-truck? Or shared the bed with two cats while trying not to overdose on Benadryl for your pet allergies? One of my clients seemed to always draw the short stick when it came to accommodations while on the road with her singing group. Now she requests a hotel room unless she personally knows the host.

I was treated to an RV camper while speaking at a women's retreat held on a working ranch. It wouldn't have been so bad, but I had to tiptoe through the "tulips" in the cattle fields separating the cabins from my RV. One horse decided to court my humble abode during the middle of the night—I awoke to the camper swaying and an odd sounding love song. Oh dear!

Travel

Being picked up at the airport by a complete stranger is doomed for mess-ups. A few of the ones I've experienced include:

- Drivers who get lost and won't allow me to help them read the map.
- Drivers with admitted vision challenges.
- A driver of the opposite sex asking me to read his sexually explicit scene in a novel to see if I think it's too edgy for the Christian conference.
- A vehicle that smelled like the residence of an elderly cat.
- Drivers who refuse to help with baggage—or doors for that matter.
- Drivers so programmed to redeem the time by picking my brain about their own projects that they made me feel like I was literally a captive audience—maybe even temporarily abducted.

Fees

Probably the #1 problem I hear from speakers is when their event planner says they will be sure to give an honorarium and mileage, and then when they hand over the check, it isn't even enough to pay for fuel. The worst time that happened to me—a pastor's wife scheduled me for her women's event, and I needed to travel 325 miles in a snowstorm. They didn't cancel the event, so I arranged for a friend with a leased SUV to drive me. I told my driver I'd give her my travel expense check to pay the mileage overage with her lease company.

The only problem? Once we drove through slush and snow and hail and ice to get there, the check didn't even quite pay for gas, let alone mileage. Funny how the word mileage can mean different things to different people. Now I use a speaker contract. I have to. It protects me and it assures the event planner that they can rely on me to supply the program for their special occasion.

Some of the other war stories I've heard regarding fees include:

1. Planners who canceled the event without paying a cancellation fee. Some even expected their deposits returned. They had no consideration for what the speaker was out, such as turning down other events for that date, or advance preparation on a custom program.

2. Speakers who had to eat the cost of airfare because the venue expected them to drive long distances to save money. Their definition of paid travel was two separate things.

3. Hosts who apologize at the end of the event for low attendance, and then explain that due to low numbers, they won't be able to pay the remainder of the honorarium due.

4. Events cancelled at the last minute due to death, illness, or weather disasters. How can you manage this in the most equitable way for the event and for you when it's due to situations outside of anyone's control? Consider writing cancellation options into your contract, such as a replacement date if the venue cancels due to an emergency, or a replacement speaker if you have to cancel at the last minute. The best option is if you can reschedule so you don't miss out on the opportunity, especially if you've already prepared speeches specifically for their assigned theme.

Different Denominations

Sometimes you will speak for events hosted by churches of different denominations than your home church. Usually this isn't a problem, but every once in a while, even though the planning committee approved you for the event, attendees will quiz you about your denominational background.

One retreat group asked me if I was scared that they were a certain denomination. I could tell they were trying to shake me. So I threw the question back to them. "I'm not scared—are you scared that I'm [my denomination]?" Then we chuckled and I promised not to touch on the ways we practice our faith differently.

There was one time in the program where the differences surfaced. They practiced the sign of the cross after every prayer. I was to lead the final prayer, and I did not want to disrespect their practices by not doing the sign of the cross, but it isn't how I personally express my prayers. Determined to end with a unified spirit rather than highlighting a way we differed, I had all the ladies hold hands as we prayed the closing prayer. This ended up being a special benediction for them, and it resolved my problem as well.

We all have speaker-related problems. It's how we deal with them that matters. And yes—later you'll even grin!

WHY WON'T THEY BOOK ME?

S ometimes you try so hard to make a big splash in the speaking
world, and you can't figure out why you aren't getting bookings.
Take this personal inventory to discover the reasons contributing to
your drought and create a new plan to get more speaking gigs. You
have to fill their demand—not demand the bookings!

Do a Personal Inventory

- **Do you practice your faith differently than the events you're targeting?** No two people worship or believe the same way, so speakers aren't expected to be spiritual clones of their hosts. But the hosts need assurance that you aren't going to lead their groups into a different direction than their church or organization sanctions.

- **Are you missing impressive endorsements?** Unless you have word of mouth and the person recommending you knows both you and the event planner, you will need endorsements that get the attention of event planners.

- **Is your honorarium too high for your level of experience or for the budget of the events you're pitching?** If you want more bookings, sometimes you'll need to come down on your honorarium, just until you get more experience. Ask the host what their usual budget is for the event and see if there's a way you can work with that.

- **Are your speaker promotions going too far away from home?** Most professional speakers want to be considered "national" speakers, traveling far and wide to tell the world our message. But many events now have to cut costs and one way they do that is to invite a speaker who doesn't require a very large travel fee. So, don't forget to promote your work close to home—or clustered close to events elsewhere that have paid your travel.

- **Do you have outdated promotional literature and online speaker page (or worse . . . missing in action)?** Keep in mind the #1 biblical marketing principle, "How will they hear unless you tell them?" Event planners can't read our minds that we want to be booked. Even if they hear about you from a friend, they want to look you up online or have print literature to which they can refer for additional information. Planning committees need details, so they can compare you to the other speakers they are considering. Give them what they need and make it top notch if you want to get the booking.

- **Have you branded yourself into such a narrow niche that event planners can't book you for general events?** Many events need a program with broad appeal.

A Sample "Brain-Tsunami"

Here's an illustration of brainstorming no-fail events to get booked. This example is for women's ministry speakers, but no matter what kind of speaker you are, you can use this example and brainstorm a formula that will work for your own type of venue.

First, consider the annual events for which your target hosts need to schedule speakers. Many women's ministry organizations have one, two, or three annual events. They include, but are not limited to:

- May Event (Mothers and all women)
- Friendship or Inspirational Event (Often their outreach event of the year)
- Christmas Event (A brunch, tea, banquet—often decorated with a theme)

Then, look over your standard talks and your brand. Even if you have a specific focus, you can create a more generalized program that will help you get more bookings. Brainstorm a program that would fit with the main events your target event planners are booking for the year. (For the women's ministry example, you would make sure you have programs that are especially suitable for the three main events mentioned above, or other types of events they tend to host.)

If you are targeting church ministries, don't be so tied to your niche that the average church won't book you. You have to be a good draw for the majority of their audience. If you're just starting out, don't assume the big churches who are looking for niche speakers will invite you. And the smaller churches need for you to take a more "general" approach. Take your brand but broaden the focus. For example, instead of speaking to stay-at-home moms, speak to all women about some of the same issues stay-at-home moms face. Or if you write for children but you want to speak to adults, think up a program that will be of interest to the typical audience receiving your promotional materials.

When doing follow-up after sending promotional information, ask the contact what events they have coming up in the next year that they haven't filled, and the goal for the event. Show how you can fill that spot and what you could do to customize it to achieve their goals.

My husband pastored churches running 100-200, so when I received a speaker packet from someone wanting to speak to mothers of young children, I couldn't invite them to come speak. I only had the budget for a general speaker who would inspire (and if I'm honest, entertain) my entire women's ministry audience. If we were a larger church, we could invite speakers in for specialty groups. This gives you an example of evaluating your lists.

If your speaking program list has niche topics, but your event planner list requires general topics, then you have just branded yourself out of speaking invitations. So, it's time to make sure your program offerings fit the venues where you're offering them!

Once you figure out a way your message fits the audience, you will have one foot in the door. Then it's up to you to learn how to follow up so that you get both feet in the door, and on up to the podium! Make it fit to make it work.

TROUBLE-SHOOTING BEFORE THERE'S TROUBLE

Every speaker faces problems during their programs. Some are preventable and some require improvisation. With advanced preparation you'll be equipped if these situations surface.

Introductions

If you've ever had an emcee struggle with introducing you to the audience, you know how awkward this can be. Put your host at ease by providing them with a printed copy of your bio. The audience wants to hear why they should stay tuned for your program, so make sure the host introduces you with a bio that is the right length and reflects the feel of the presentation.

Recently a host ignored my printed bio and chose to research me online. She found old news that was no longer accurate. I should have had a current one to hand her at the event rather than rely on the earlier e-mailed speaker pack I sent her.

Microphone/Sound System Problems

Probably every speaker has a sound system nightmare they can share. It starts with the microphones. Who thinks of the mic pack when selecting an outfit for the event? It only takes one time of dealing with a roaming mic pack to be sure to wear a 2-piece outfit so you can clip the battery to the waistband and fish the cord up through your top to clip it on the lapel. Or use the countryman style headset microphone.

Of course, there are more sound system woes than I have space to discuss. Animated speakers hate being tied down behind the lectern, but if there's no cordless mic, you might be anchored to one spot with the podium mic. Or perhaps you have to mess with a handheld microphone because the batteries ran out for the lapel mic. I won't even get into the gremlins that can enter the sound system, or the inexperienced sound techs who sometimes get recruited to run the control panel.

Or if it's a women's event, the times a wife of a sound tech runs the equipment so it's an all-women event (that whole Girl Power thing). It's not a bad deal unless the spouse has never been trained to run the audiovisual system knowing what to do if there are squeals, hums, or no sound at all. The moral of the story is to be prepared. Duct tape and batteries don't hurt, either!

At one event I had a holstered mic pack on each hip—one for recording purposes, one for in-house audio. I was hooked up prior to the meal so they could do a sound check. I didn't plan ahead for the restroom break I took between the meal and my program. I learned I'm not adept at holding two mic packs while taking care of the restroom calisthenics. Now I know the importance of timing when I get wired for sound.

Feedback

Sometimes we get the wrong kind of feedback when we're speaking—squeals, pops, and sound distortions. If this happens, keep speaking as you assess the problem. Walk away from speakers or monitors and move the mic to the proper distance. Make sure jewelry isn't brushing across a lapel mic. Pay attention to the hand signals coming from your sound technician.

I know some speakers who bring their own mic to avoid problems. Some are Bluetooth enabled, with no cord or battery pack to fight. Others are the countryman style over-ear face mic that can be fitted to the contour of your face if it's your own, rather than using the one they give you that has been used by others prior to this event. (I groan to think of the germs a non-sanitized mic delivers.)

And the last idea should be first—before you speak, spend time praying over the entire program, including the sound system.

Projected Visual Materials

Be prepared to present your program without multi-media projected on the screen, in case something keeps you from using it. Don't rely on the screen for your notes or to make the impact for you—your words need to stand up on their own. If something happens during the program, don't spend time trying to fix the problem—that will cause your speaking momentum to fizzle. Instead, move forward with the least distracting solution possible.

Notes

There are several challenges to prevent as far as our speaking notes go. It's a nightmare to witness our note cards or sheets of paper fly off the podium. Another challenge is being unable to see the notes due to the lighting or the size of the print. To manage these potential problems, I recommend using a 3-ring notebook. Print notes in a font you can easily read. Use 14-point size font if the 12-point size is too small. I select the font Arial Rounded MT Bold because it's easy to read, and I set my margins differently on each edge to position as many words as possible on a page without going below my sight line or too close to the binder rings (Top: .5", Left: 1.5", Right: .5", Bottom: 1.5"). Punch holes and put in a 3-ring binder. Print your logo and slide it in the front cover of the notebook.

An electronic tablet can be used at the podium for your notes. There is a teleprompter app that allows the notes to scroll with your personal pacing. If you do this, have a paper version too, just in case the unthinkable happens and the tablet doesn't work.

How can you prevent forgetting your notes at home? Always have your program on a thumb drive, burned to a CD, or bring your computer or tablet with you. I usually bring my laptop because there are times I'm asked to speak on something extra to fill in at the last minute. All my notes from previous presentations and articles come in handy for emergency requests. Another way to keep from forgetting your notes at home is to have a consistent packing routine so that you know exactly where your speaking notes are as you check off your packing list. I have a special place for my notes in my carry-on rolling business organizer, so I always check to make sure it's there before I leave home.

Cold Audience

We rely on instant feedback from the audience to spur us on during our programs. Seeing the facial expressions, body language, or hearing verbal affirmation assures us the program is hitting home. What about the times when the audience is not receptive?

Find a few familiar faces in the crowd and feed off of their positive body language so the negative vibes from others doesn't distract you. Insert a personal illustration if you notice the mood is sagging. Transparency is refreshing and relatable so it will add an instant boost to the atmosphere in the room. You can even insert humor as long as it doesn't sound canned or corny.

Also, realize various cultures and traditions respond differently to messages, so don't assume they dislike your presentation just because they don't react the same as others. And sometimes, there is spiritual resistance going on, and before the end of your time there, you get to experience an incredible break-through. Continue with your part of the program and trust the rest to God.

Dry Mouth

Many conditions cause dry mouth symptoms for speakers. Nerves alone can cause a temporary reduction in salivary flow. I have Sjogren's syndrome, which attacks the salivary glands. When speakers experience dryness, lips smack, tongues stick to mouth roofs, teeth even stick to lips. It's not only annoying, it can prevent a speaker from enunciating well. If you suffer from this, find a solution that works for you. Some hosts set water at the podium, but if they do not, bring your own to sip at appropriate times.

Try products designed for entertainers and dry mouth sufferers. Do not chew gum. Instead, tuck a tiny sugar-free mint in-between the upper teeth and the lining of the cheek. Consider putting a light film of petroleum jelly on your teeth to prevent them from sticking to your lips. Worst-case, try biting your tongue. This stimulates the salivary flow.

Prepare in advance for dry mouth by drinking a steaming cup of Throat Coat tea. The slippery elm in it keeps the mucosa of your mouth and throat lubricated much longer than simple water does. (If you want to try this tea, be sure to check with your physician first.) There are also throat sprays you can use before going on stage such as Entertainer's Secret.

Be prepared for these emergencies before they happen, and you'll be ready for whatever comes your way on the speaking trail.

Time Limits

Often, a program that involves more than our talk ends up going long before we ever get up to the podium to speak. As we get ready to go up on stage, the host asks us in a whisper if we can adjust the length of our message. Other times, we aren't asked to reduce our time, but we feel the pressure of dismissing at the expected time. What do we do? How can we keep our good name by honoring time restraints when other parts of the program have crowded into our time?

I once was asked to deliver a one-hour program to a professional group. To prepare for the presentation, I invited four women to come up and allow me to use them as demonstrations as I trained the audience. I prepped each of them, and they anticipated being a part of this special hour. Only one problem. It ended up not being an hour. The emcee responsible for introducing me used a third of my time to give his own inspirational message to the crowd. I guess he figured he had control of the lectern and a captive audience. That left me with only 40 minutes to deliver a 60-minute program.

Normally I would have omitted one of my key points, but I couldn't do that since I had invited these four women to come be a part of the presentation. I'm not great at math, but it was easy to figure if I removed five minutes from each of the four sections, that would make up the twenty minutes I lost.

The founder of the organization thanked me for helping them get back on schedule. And several from the audience pulled me aside one-on-one to mention the same thing—they thought it was an act of grace to not bemoan the lengthy introduction and to do my part to give a quality program in a reduced amount of time. And when people witness grace, they are drawn in. On the other hand, the same people realized my emcee was showboating, and he risked getting fewer invitations for his own speaking engagements with this group due to his inconsideration of the time allotted him.

Get Back on Track

One of the best ways you can endear yourself to an event coordinator is to get their entire day's schedule back on track by adjusting the time you spend on your part of the program. Consider it a challenge or a game, to see how much valuable content you can say in a short amount of time. Give them the important parts to chew on, but don't speed up so much they feel overloaded by too much material. Our brains can only absorb a limited amount of information per minute. And pace it with something light to offset the heavy dose of info-dump. Use your best story or illustration from the presentation but omit some of the others. Filler is the first thing to go when determining what to present.

If you have four main points, perhaps you can do just two or three points and leave one or two off. You can offer to e-mail additional points for your talk to the attendees if they come visit your table and sign-up for your mailing list. Then send them your full presentation if you like. By doing this, you turn a negative situation into a positive.

In addition to asking the emcee or event director how long you have to speak, ask when they want you to conclude your part of the program. This will help you know when you must cut off. Look at the clock when they introduce you and tabulate how long you have. You can make it work, and they will thank you for it!

Grace Time

One time I was given the program way late, and the host announced to the audience as she introduced me that since we were delayed due to situations outside of my control, they were going to extend the program an extra half hour. She explained that they had prayed for God to make a way to have me there and prayed that whole year for God to put together the material for my presentation. They felt it would be cheating God's purpose to diminish the time for the main part of the program. By prepping the audience that they would get more value by extending the time, the audience didn't give me daggers with their eyes as I spoke!

Even though I had permission to go my regular length with the program, I removed some of the filler so that they got out quicker than they expected. This is the only time, though, that the host offered my full time when they were behind on the rest of the program. Most tend to expect the speaker to be the one to delete part of the program. (My preference would be to cut back on announcements, thank-yous, and perhaps a song—but everyone is different!)

Another way to reduce the length of your presentation is to use fewer Scriptures than originally planned. Cut out longer portions and give a summary. Be sure to still use some Scripture if it is an inspirational message because it is the Word of God that has the power to change lives.

Event coordinators tell me about a different issue they have regarding a speaker's time allotment. Some speakers take longer than what they've been given. If a host tells you to take however long God leads you to speak—press them for a more specific time to shut down (allowing flexibility of course if God is at work and impresses you to go a bit longer).

Even when hosts say they don't mind, attendees do have a limit to what they can take in. The brain can only process information as long as the bottom can tolerate sitting. Other situations might also cause the audience to become restless, so look for the cues that it's time to wrap up your presentation. Some distractions include: a room that is too hot or too cold, crying babies, loud kitchen help, or street noise. Don't be one of those speakers who takes longer than he or she should to present the message.

Distractions and Emergencies

Speaking of distractions, not many programs survive unscathed by distractions. Cell phones ring, babies cry, and medical emergencies happen. How you manage the distractions from the stage sets the tone for the entire group. Most issues are best handled by the event team, positioned behind the audience. It's usually better for the speaker to continue with the message rather than drawing more attention to the problem.

What should you do if the electricity goes out?

Normally the host will speak up and tell you whether you should attempt to continue the program, but if not, assess if there are any risks of continuing without electricity. When this has happened to me, I've stepped down off of the stage and gotten closer to the audience and spoken in my best projecting voice possible. If it's going to be a long day of programs, I'll ask the host to find out how long the outage might be so we can make any adjustments necessary to the schedule. And if all else fails, suggest a restroom break so the planners can work on a Plan B.

What to do if someone passes out or has a medical emergency?

If someone slumps over, passed out—everyone is concerned. It's difficult to continue the program and expect the audience to focus on the message. Better to stop, acknowledge someone has a health situation being tended to by staff. As long as you see someone is addressing the medical needs, you can continue with the program.

Sometimes you have the only view of the audience so you might have to call attention to the individual who needs help. Make sure they ask for medical help in the group if needed or call 9-1-1 if deemed appropriate. Announce that it's important for the patient to have space and air. If you sense God nudging you to stop and have group prayer for the one afflicted, do so.

Sometimes this can be the most powerful moment of an event—combining hearts and hands to pray for someone suddenly suffering.

What to do if a storm hits?

Use weather wisdom regarding storms. If it's a nice steady rain and the electricity is still on, then there's usually no reason to discontinue the program—although the sound of rain on the roof might be a bit distracting. If there's a tornado, have the host come to the podium to announce a safe place for attendees to relocate. This happened the weekend my husband and I candidated for our first ministry position at a church. It left a big impression on us as we all crammed into a basement area while the tornado sirens blared in the church parking lot.

Use wisdom when announcing if people should be out on the roads or if they should stay put. Another factor to be aware of is flash flooding. If you are located in an area that might get flooded, keeping people from making it home, you might need to dismiss the group earlier than expected so they are safe on the roads before the floods rise.

What to do if some sort of fight breaks out?

Very rarely a personality clash can escalate into a verbal or even physical altercation. If this happens, motion to the host or security to escort the distraction away from the auditorium.

The Show Must Go On!

There's nothing worse than expecting the show to go on regardless of the circumstances. Sometimes it is in how you respond to the challenge that impacts the audience most of all. Use these unique situations to allow God to work in a way tailor-made for the occasion. Be flexible!

PREVENTING CONTRACT CONFLICTS

I've talked with several speakers over the past year who tell me war stories of conflicts with event planners regarding details of their booking agreements. Some had written contracts, some had verbal contracts, and some admit they didn't nail down many of the details. Most speakers who have contracts will tell you they came up with their contract wording based on agreements gone wrong with previous bookings.

Even though it feels uncomfortable to ask for a signed contract in Christian circles, there's much more discomfort to *not* have one and then have a problem arise. But I admit to going both ways with this—the main thing is to communicate all the details ahead of time to prevent issues from arising.

When you have a contract, it's nice to talk through it during the time you're discussing the booking with the event planner. That way rather than bringing up subjects that make you squirm you can tell them you're just filling out the details of the contract. It's sad that talking about our needs makes us feel like we're being demanding when it's simply taking care of business. I think this is especially difficult for women who want to avoid coming across like they think they're "all that" or a diva.

If it's still a struggle for you to talk line by line through the contract when making the booking, then you need to hire a booking agent to do this part for you. It protects your interests, and delivers a better outcome for the event, too.

Don't assume the event planners know what is considered standard for bringing in an outside speaker. This might be their first time. Many of them want to do what is right—they're simply unsure what that is. It's our job to guide them and show them what to consider. It not only prevents unrealistic and unmet expectations, it helps their future speakers to have an easier time of discussing their contracts.

Details to Cover During the "Talk"

- Contact person
- Contact information
- Name of organization
- Location of event
- Date of event
- Arrival time/departure time
- Travel accommodations (flying, driving, details)
- Meals and lodging
- Travel expense
- Honorarium
- Deposit
- Program title/Speaking topic(s)
- Number of presentations
- Number of attendees expected
- Audio-visual needs
- Cancellation policy
- Product table set-up and assistance
- Additional notes/needs

You may think some of those details aren't important, but they are! Here are some problems speakers have shared with me, due to not having the expectations in print:

Expected to Be at Event Overnight

A retreat booked a speaker to only deliver a presentation on one day of the event, so the speaker made plans accordingly. Except the event planner had not voiced their expectation for the speaker to be there the other day of the retreat, to encourage attendees and be available for counsel. The event team expected the speaker to pay for her own lodging, thinking it was a "treat" for the speaker to come to the retreat without having to pay for the full program.

Expected to Come for Gas Money Only

An event said they were taking care of travel expenses, but these were not spelled out in advance. The speaker thought that meant mileage plus meals on the road. The event planner meant gas money.

Expected to Do More than Speak

A retreat planning team meant for the speaker to be the whole program. Games, skits, discussion questions, prayer time, music time, you name it. But they assumed the speaker knew this. The speaker brought three speaking programs, but nothing else. The retreat was left scrambling to fill the extra time for the two-day retreat.

Expected to Cancel Due to Low Registrations

Some venues cancel if they don't make goal on the number of registrations, due to budget issues. That is why it's necessary for speakers to ask for a deposit and cancelation policy agreed upon in advance. More work is done by the speaker before the event than at the event, and they should be compensated for their time, even if the event doesn't materialize.

A deposit secures the date, because a booking keeps the speaker from booking elsewhere. Often a deposit is 50 percent of the honorarium. Others ask for all their travel expense up front plus 10 percent of their honorarium. You set your deposit based on your needs, to protect the time you've invested in their event, and also create a refund policy.

If you're uncomfortable asking for a deposit, at least consider doing this if they have requested a new topic you must research and prepare for in advance. You will have a lot of time invested in their program and may never use that topic again.

Expected Speaker to Share Room

Lodging details can be difficult to discuss if it's not part of the contract. Don't assume the host will put you up somewhere nice, in your own room, unless you spell that out in the contract and during the discussion. When some hosts say they will "put you up for the night" they mean they have a volunteer who will host you. Sometimes this works out to be the best haven of rest you've ever experienced, and other times this means you're sharing a room with little Johnny or Sara, and their three cats. (You're allergic.)

I've also heard of retreats and conferences where the speakers are expected to have roommates—sometimes another speaker (can be great for fellowship). But sometimes it's a conferee who feels like they have their own private time for a consultation or counseling session with you. Discuss what the lodging provisions are, and if you aren't agreeable to them, explain why.

As I explained in another part of the book, I was secluded in an RV a half-mile from the lodge on a ranch because they thought I'd want alone time. While they meant well, I would have preferred the fellowship of the other women to being so isolated. Other times, I do prefer to have my own room apart from the group so I can pray and prepare my heart for the ministry of the event.

The bottom line is this: we all have different needs and expectations. Manage those expectations while negotiating the details of the event, by using a written contract. Or at least follow up on a phone conversation by sending an e-mail spelling out the details discussed during the call. This can be used later if there are any disputes regarding your agreement.

THE FUZZY/FOGGY EVENT PLANNER

How do you deal with a floundering event planner? Maybe she's fuzzy or foggy or flakey. It's our job as professional speakers to put everyone at ease—the leadership and the audience. We have to make the best of challenging situations and learn from them for the next time. I'll tell you my story with Mrs. Planner and then we can brainstorm preventative measures.

Event Dilemma

Mrs. P invited me to speak for her women's retreat. She knows me from an association of churches to which we both belonged. She gave me the topic of the retreat and told me the other speaker would talk about health issues, so she'd like me to talk about something else. She asked for my bio so she could promote the retreat but didn't want a descriptive topic blurb.

I sent her my bio at several word counts so she could pick what fit her needs best. I figured one would be ideal for the print materials and a different one might be preferred when she introduced me to the audience.

Over the next six months, I didn't receive any more information, which I needed to promote the retreat to my own women's group. We never saw any advance literature about it. I wasn't even sure if it was still scheduled, since we were supposed to be one of the groups attending.

About three weeks before the event, a volunteer from the group made an announcement about the event during our church service and offered brochures if anyone was interested. (Surprise!) She said only two women had registered so she hoped we would all sign up. I asked for a brochure.

My bio had been rewritten so it no longer matched my branding platform. It mentioned my health story—the very thing she suggested I stay away from in my talk! I e-mailed the event planner for clarification. She said I could speak on anything I wanted and was very accommodating. She mentioned that the other two ladies had never spoken in public before. Thinking it might be best to put the experienced speaker last on the schedule, I ended up with the spot where the ladies were sleepy, hungry, restless, and wanting to get on the road. They gave me a full hour to speak. I can *fill* an hour, but I know how much I squirm when I'm in the audience for such a long day of speakers.

The event planner mentioned the low registrations. I'm not a prideful person, but the publicist in me wondered if the retreat could have been promoted better by advertising my accomplishments since the other speakers were newbies. Instead they made my bio the shortest and didn't mention I was a national speaker.

Then, less than a week prior to the event the director e-mailed me again to warn me that another speaker had a family emergency and might cancel. She asked if I could speak twice if needed. We discussed options and decided instead to add more interactive components to the program to help the audience stay alert. I found out two days before the event that the other speaker did cancel, and she needed me to stretch my program. A day before the event the new schedule came and I was assigned 90 minutes.

The retreat did get a few more registrations and it went well except for two issues. The emcee didn't introduce me to the audience and didn't mention the schedule changes. Afterward, a couple of the ladies kidded me for being so long-winded. They had no way of knowing I actually let them out ten minutes early.

Fortunately, God was still God over the event and lots of good God-stuff happened. We all had a fun time. I came home brainstorming what I could have done differently to make it an even better event. I share my ponderings here, in case it helps you with preventative maintenance.

What to do when...
- they change your bio?
- they change your topic?
- they don't keep you informed about the event?
- they don't promote the event?
- they change the time allotted to your part of the event?
- they don't inform the audience what to expect?

Solutions:
- Ask for clarification.
- Be ready for compromise.
- Offer assistance to promote the event if it's open to the public.
- Suggest added components to stretch a program, such as a no-rehearsal skit, a fun interactive motion-song, a discussion question (fun or serious) for each table, volunteers to read portions so they hear other voices than your own, etc.
- Add extra humor to cover any awkward moments (as long as it is natural).
- Work in such a way that you don't make the planner look incompetent even though she's not been on her game for the event.
- Introduce yourself to the audience by telling a story, so they learn who you are without it sounding like you are bragging on yourself.

- Begin your time by telling the audience what your part of the program will look like so they have the right frame of reference for how much time it will take.
- Make sure you have enough promotional materials to give each attendee a copy. That will fill in what they didn't get from the missing emcee introduction.

I'll let you in on a little secret that worked to endear me to the audience. I told them I was very aware of the rule that "tired rears make for tired ears." The listener can only take in what the seat can endure. Then I explained that I found a remedy for it…chocolate. We distributed two kinds of chocolate to each table and gave them a chocolate break in the middle of my program. Sometimes a planned interruption goes a long way in keeping their attention to the very end.

DEALING WITH CLING-ONS

S peakers are at risk for attracting what I call cling-ons. These are broken people who aren't stable enough to respect proper relationship boundaries. There are different types of cling-ons, and it's good to be alert to these dysfunctional audience members so we know how best to help them while protecting our own personal space.

Crushes

If you've served in the public eye for any time at all, you probably have your own story of a person from the opposite sex developing a crush on you. I've had a few of these, even though they are fully aware of my happy marriage. Some have even met my husband, yet still ask if they can call to talk to me outside the realm of appropriate professional interaction or Christian fellowship.

I've evaluated what causes such a crush phenomenon, since I'm no trophy, and I think it's because I show others I believe in them. I stir up their creativity, help them dream again, and inspire them to achieve great things for God. Because inspirational speakers stir up passions, people have renewed hopes and want to be around us more. Their stimulated emotions confuse them into thinking it is a romantic connection.

Once I had a gentleman say he wanted to move to my town and asked if I'd help him make plans. The problem? He lived five states away and didn't know another soul in my region. No—this was not going to happen and I had to be very firm to dissuade him. After that, I let him know if he needed anything from my communications business, my business manager at the time (who happened to be my spouse) would help him.

When he continued to contact me after business hours and without appointments, I let him know I could no longer help him. My refusal did not stop him. Caller identification helped me avoid his phone calls. When he left voicemails I didn't return his calls. And I didn't reply to his e-mails either. It took a while, but he eventually gave up. I'll be honest—it pains me to do that. I'm not a cold person, but he misunderstood any attention as special affection, so I had to be firm.

It's not difficult for audiences to find our contact information. Ask God to help you identify any individuals who have developed an unhealthy attraction to you.

Advice-Seekers

Troubled men and women often approach us after our programs. Part of the reason we do what we do in our speaking careers is to minister to those looking for answers. But there's no way we can provide in-depth counseling during brief one-on-one sessions while others are waiting in line to visit with us. The ones who cling on the most have probably already bent the ears of family, friends, neighbors, co-workers, church leaders, and others. They might even believe we're their last hope.

Some will pick up our business cards and contact us later. When you receive these sorts of e-mails, notes, and phone calls, say a quick prayer asking God for wisdom in your dealings with this individual. God can guide you in knowing how much time is healthy to spend with advice-seekers. If you discern any red flags, have an exit plan in place. Some speakers have a standard reply to cling-ons, recommending they contact their local minister or counselor for ongoing needs. Tell them your busy speaking ministry isn't designed to counsel individuals after events end.

It will be hard for them to accept your refusal to help. You were so nice at the program. They are certain you can rescue them. And you are nice—but some seekers you can never help enough—they will expect more and more of your time and attention.

Wanna-Bees

Wanna-bees make up another type of annoying groupie. These are individuals who listen to you give your presentation, and think to themselves, "I could do what she does." The really bold ones come and tell you they think that! It's fine if it stops there, but some push you to tell them how they can get where you are. They want you to take them under your wings to mentor, to spoon-feed them with information, even to share your contacts so they can match your speaking bookings.

I had a lady who wouldn't take no for an answer. She was convinced my sole purpose was to launch her speaking and writing ministry. She stalked me. When I ministered to other individuals, she found a way to be in our personal space, intruding on our private conversations. Each time she did this, it was such an uncomfortable invasion, the ones talking to me left. Multiple times she asked, "So when are you going to launch my career?" It was very uncomfortable, and I had to reinforce my boundaries by telling her I was not taking on new coaching clients due to my busy schedule. This not only said, "No," but also showed her I don't work for free. It's my business. (I do sometimes feel led to mentor someone at no cost, but God makes those arrangements, not the interested party.)

The key to these uncomfortable situations is to develop your own policies, your own boundaries, and your own exit plan. Be wise in your dealings, always staying in public places during interactions with them. Pay attention to your gut feelings—God often gives us a sixth sense to protect us. Just because God calls us to love everyone doesn't mean we have to let them into our personal spaces. It's called personal for a reason!

BEFORE (AND AFTER) SICK DAYS DERAIL YOU

I t never fails—when an event date approaches, the speaker has something unexpected come up. Often, it's a health issue. What can you do to prepare in advance for possible sick days so that when they surface you aren't derailed?

Health Boosters
We all have weak links to do with our physical health. Anytime we're under additional stress, reduced sleep, or exposed to other triggers, these susceptible areas are at risk for being exacerbated. A few possibilities include: migraines, back pain, gastrointestinal problems, autoimmune issues, allergies, etc. Stay in tune to what your weak spots are so you can be prepared to deal with them if they flare up.

Since sleep and stress have a lot to do with almost every health condition, at the bare minimum, make sure you are dealing appropriately with these. And build up the proper balance in your immune system (not depleted, not hyperactive) by eating and exercising the best way for your personal health plan. It's not the time right before a big event to change up your medical regimen or forget to take your medications or supplements. Consistency is key.

I know a few speakers who throw away good health by going on a near hunger strike prior to an event, not for spiritual reasons, but in order to fit into a coveted outfit. Not smart if that lack of eating causes you to cancel the event. You won't get to enjoy your fancy wardrobe if you're home sick now, will you?

What other general precautions can you take ahead of time to try to prevent a medical issue cropping up when you have a speaking gig?

Prayer Boosters

As covered in another section, prayer is a great resource. When it comes to preventing sickness or praying you feel better if you're already sick—prayer plays a big part in seeing you are on the road to recovery before you're on the road to your speaking event. So if you experience any niggles hinting you might be getting sick or feeling poorly, activate your prayer team, your church prayer chain, your social networking buddies—anyone who cares enough to pray—get them praying so you are strong enough to speak at the event.

Travel Boosters

Sometimes, we feel fine when we leave home, but something happens along the way that causes us to wind up at the event in less than excellent health. What are some problem areas to avoid when traveling to prevent triggering health issues?

- Avoid the extremes of early morning or late-night flights if it takes you out of your normal waking and sleep times.

- Don't try to carry too much. Even with rolling bags we can twist our backs out of alignment if we try to juggle too much baggage.

- Remember to pack your medications where you can get to them in-flight. Sometimes we leave home fine but arrive at the event with symptoms due to missing important medications.

- Allow plenty of time for layovers between flights so you

don't have to run through the airport. I've ended up with twisted ankles, spasming back muscles, bleeding blisters, crashing blood sugar and more, all because of that mad dash between flights to board the next plane.

- Travel the day prior, if you know you need more time to bounce back before you speak. This will allow you to be fresh for the big day.

- Consider the environment where you are traveling— especially if it's different than your hometown. I tend to have more illness if I'm in high altitudes, dry climates, moldy surfaces, dusty-windy areas, etc. Know what your triggers are and prepare in advance for them. For many ailments, simply keeping hydrated is the key (drink more water, use eye and nose drops, etc.).

Plan B

There are times when you determine you aren't sick enough to stay home, but you will need to make adjustments if you go. Perhaps you need to avoid the socialization hours, but you can show up for the speaking program.

One time I twisted my ankle and broke my heel the night before a conference. I ended up in the ER twice and at a surgeon once while away from home! But with a little creativity, my part of the conference was able to carry on without much of a blip on the radar.

We secured a wheelchair from the host church and I taught at the day seminar on Saturday, seated in the wheelchair. I rested on Sunday and didn't go out with the faculty to church or the restaurant. On Monday and Tuesday I stayed in the faculty lounge and prayed for the other aspects of the conference with my foot propped up—different speakers took my spots when the subjects were versatile enough for them to cover. I ventured out at lunchtime to interact with the conferees and to answer questions pertaining to my specialty. Then on Wednesday I presented one of the final sessions from my wheelchair, covering a subject that fell in my area of expertise. This was the best way we could work with what seemed like an impossible situation.

And then there's the worst-case scenario—when you realize there's nothing you can do but stay home due to a health emergency. Sometimes you have to cancel due to your own health, or in order to help an ill family member. I'm not sure who is shaken more when this realization hits—the event planner or the speaker! I've been on both ends of this, and it's never easy. What are some ways you can plan ahead when you need Plan B to cover emergency cancellations?

Here are a few ideas:

- Have a back-up speaker who is available to come—or to connect via a video call to provide a program.

- Graduate another speaker at the event from breakout session to keynote speaker.

- Reschedule a date if there's enough notice.

- Utilize someone who has been on the planning or prayer team, who has the heartbeat of the event, to fill in.

- Share notes if requested, so the fill-in speaker isn't left scrambling at the last minute. (This isn't the time to get stingy with your proprietary information.)

I've heard story after story about how God used medical issues in some way for a great outcome at a speaking event. Sometimes he leads speakers to conduct the event even if they are sick, lifted up from the support of others partnering in prayer. There are incredible reports of times when symptoms shut off as speakers step up on stage and return after they make their closing remarks. Other times the symptoms stay gone for good. Either way, the power of God sits atop the speaker and is actively at work.

If the symptoms are not alleviated, God can still use the circumstances in some way to bring about a positive result. And sometimes, the symptoms are bad enough the speaker has to go with Plan B and nothing takes God by surprise. It was his Plan A all along.

I wonder if these situations arise because we simply need to be reminded that God is in control. It's not about us, it's about him. When symptoms flare, the circumstances require us to trust him more and lean on him for wisdom and for strength. And often, how we interact with him before and during an event is more important than what we planned on saying during the program. That's what leads to lasting differences in us and in the lives of others.

THE PHYSICALLY CHALLENGED SPEAKER

At a recent writers' conference I briefly mentioned a physical struggle during my keynote. After the program, several conferees asked me to elaborate more on dealing with health issues as a communicator. Many had given up the idea of being a speaker because they thought their health would be too much of a drawback or distraction. My challenge to you is this: if God allows you to deal with a medical condition and also has called you to speak, don't you think he might like to actually use your struggles rather than disqualify you from being a speaker?

Think of the people in the Bible who said they could not speak due to a physical ailment. God used them anyway. Having a medical condition isn't a *Get-out-of-speaking* card!

While it's possible to be a speaker despite your condition, you will be challenged to deal with difficulties others don't have. But you can also offer a unique depth of wisdom and life experience. God wants to use you exactly how you are, and even though your diagnoses tag along, they don't have to define you. Let's talk about some specific issues.

Fatigue

No matter what your diagnosis, it's possible you struggle with fatigue. One of the best ways to deal with fatigue is to prevent it from happening. For speakers, this might mean:

- Traveling a day or two before the event, to allow some bounce-back time.
- Insisting on going to bed earlier than normal the night before a speaking event. Some speakers take a sleep-aid and others have sleep hygiene practices.
- Bringing your CPAP or BiPAP machine along.
- Scheduling your speaking events with buffer time in-between for recuperation.
- Eating better nutrition.
- Consuming a boost of caffeine—although it's best not to abuse this or you'll have the boomerang effect.

Compromised Immune System

I have a dysfunctional immune system that, when combined with other factors, causes me to get sick more often than others. And I get a more severe case of whatever I pick up than those who shared it with me. So what do you do? Live in a bubble? Some might have to, but I'm not to that point. I simply pay attention to my surroundings. If I touch something someone else touched, I disinfect my hands. I don't hug anyone who is coughing or sick. I refuse transportation with someone who is ill. I avoid shaking hands in receiving lines—or if I do, I go wash my hands thoroughly after I'm done.

If I think I'm coming down with something, I've learned how to nip it in the bud (for the most part). Do your due diligence if you have a low immune system, and you can avoid picking up all of the bugs going around.

Food Issues

If you have food issues, don't wait for the host to ask what you can or cannot eat. Instead, as soon as you book the event let them know of any true health-related dining requirements. Don't get bogged down telling them what your food preferences are (unless they ask). If they can accommodate your nutritional needs, that's great.

Also let your host know if the time you eat is important. There have been several times when dinner was planned for 9pm, after the event, but they didn't plan on all the time needed to clear out the venue (people and decorations). So it was 10pm when I finally received food, and it wasn't all that nourishing because dining choices were limited at that time of night. One time they didn't feed me at all, so I asked my driver to stop at a convenience store on the way back to the hotel. I've learned to bring enough healthy snacks to tide me over in case their meals don't work out.

Another factor besides the logistics of avoiding foods that make you sick is dealing with how others respond to your food choices. It's best to not make a big deal of it and focus on other discussion topics. If you spotlight your limitations you will get unwanted advice, judgmental looks, and make others feel uncomfortable eating something you can't eat.

Dry Mouth

I personally deal with medically induced dry mouth. It's a struggle because if I drink too often while speaking, others assume it's due to nerves. But I can't have my tongue stick to the roof of my mouth, or have a tooth catch my inner cheek! There are times I mention it briefly at the beginning of my talk, inviting them to "drink up" whenever I take a sip due to my health condition, and then we have fun lifting our water bottles a couple of times during the presentation. It works for me!

Standing and Walking Problems

Some conditions make it difficult to walk or stand. How does this affect you as a speaker? It's uncomfortable to travel—and pain makes it harder to concentrate. Standing behind a podium is a struggle. Navigating a widespread campus to get from class to class is tough. What can you do?

Don't be embarrassed to ask for help, or to use special aids to make standing or walking easier. Ask for assistance at the airport rather than walking from security to gate. Use a wheelchair or knee scooter to get from place to place. Teach from a barstool rather than stand. Or you might want to try an AFO (Ankle Foot Orthosis) splint to help with standing.

Appearance

Some people worry about how their medical condition makes them appear. I have a sunburn-like blush that involves my face, ears, neck and chest. It looks like I'm flushed with nerves, but it's just one of my red-hot spells! I could put on red-blocking makeup, but it's so thick that my skin can't breathe and then I really *would* be red hot! (I use special corrective concealer when the condition is more than momentary.) Sometimes the best way to treat the problem is to not look at it as a problem. Others will give the benefit of the doubt (or they won't—and either way you can't fix it). I use humor a great deal to get past the issue and get on to the actual presentation.

And that's my final advice. Make the program about the message, not about the medical condition (unless that's the topic of your talk). Don't let your condition hinder you from speaking. When you use your words effectively, they won't care about the rest.

6 DANGERS OF
THE SPEAKING BIZ

As public speakers, we deal with many dangers. Not necessarily the kind that will kill us, but the kind that threatens to kill our speaking business. Be aware of these and manage them appropriately, so that you can see your business thrive.

#1-The Danger of Over-Communicating

We've all sat through programs where the speaker droned on and on and on for what seemed like hours. What makes some programs seem so long and others seem like they finished before they ever started?

What about those speakers who cram too much information into a single message and it blows the minds (not in a good way) of the listeners? Can too much content overwhelm audiences?

What about speakers who use so much PowerPoint, audiences feel they are in a two-ring circus? Or they distribute interactive hand-outs with fill-in-the-blanks but create too much note-taking work so the listener can't really absorb the message and enjoy it.

Evaluate Your Presentation in Advance

To avoid over-communicating, look over your notes ahead of time with these questions in mind.

- Does it have too many points? Excessive points make it difficult for the audience to remember the main ideas.

- Does it have too much serious material? What can be done to lighten heavier messages? It's okay to address serious subjects or have sad stories, but be sure to balance it with lighter material so it doesn't create a dark cloud over the entire presentation.

- Do you have so many notes that it's going to be a lengthy session? Better to take some of the material out of the presentation and print it up as bonus material to give them than to go long.

- What can be done to make the time seem to go faster? Try involving the audience more by asking questions or get volunteers to read portions of the notes or Bible verses. Make the program more interactive and audiences will not mind how long it goes.

At the Event

- Can you read body language to see if your points are hitting home?

- Can you tell if you need to insert some humor or some breathing room?

- Can you learn to be sensitive about your pacing and the pitch of your voice?

If you leave them wanting more—excited about the time they invested to attend—they will remember your name. If you left a bad taste in their mouths, they still might remember you, but not in a good way.

The bottom line is this: you don't need to tell them everything you know!

#2–The Danger of Me

So much of what I suggest you do to be a successful speaker forces you to focus on self. You build your platform, your bio, your website. You focus on your strengths, your selling points, your smiling photos. But there is a danger in this—creating a diva or divo in you. That is not my design or desire. As you've worked on creating your public speaking persona you might have forgotten the reason for speaking in the first place, and instead learned to like the spotlight. Now it's time to move off the stage and allow the message to be in the spotlight. Make the motive be about the audience—what do they get from hearing the message? For some speakers, they need to repeat often, "It's not about me."

Resist turning your speech into a mini (or maxi) autobiography. Even some of your most lifechanging moments don't need to be in every speech you give. You risk sounding like a broken record with an "I" problem.

Do you have the humility and the restraint to resist bragging during your speeches? Often we speak of our accomplishments as a way to make sure they know we are experts, or to overcompensate for a shortcoming of some kind—but puffing-up is off-putting. Listeners relate more to the flaws we point out in our lives, not the perfections.

#3–The Danger of Lack of Planning

Speakers are at risk for having to improvise speaking content during the actual presentation if they procrastinated too much during their prep time. Maybe this is called winging it because it's done on the fly! No one is good enough to work up brand new material while at the podium. It takes preparation.

Earn your honorarium by respecting the invitation to speak to their audience—respect starts with preparing an appropriate message. Yes, you can repeat speeches more than once, but you never want it to seem like you are calling it in by not putting effort into customizing material for your audience. Of course, you will have some impromptu moments when God brings something to mind during the delivery of your message, but don't rely on that. Do your homework!

#4–The Danger of False Advertisement

One of the top complaints regarding breakout sessions at seminars and retreats is that the session was nothing like the descriptive blurb in the schedule or program. Attendees feel like the speaker did the old bait-and-switch routine. Often this happens because we have to submit our speaker blurbs to the coordinator well ahead of the event. Between the time we write the description and the time we get to the event, our presentation has morphed into something so different it's barely recognizable from the original topic description.

Be sure to stay true to whatever has been advertised and if you can't do that, then ask the host if you can insert a new blurb into the registration materials when you first arrive to the conference, and when they introduce the breakout speakers, mention the change in the program. If they have to register in advance to attend your session, then it's essential you deliver what they expect. In fact, it's always better to under-promise and over-deliver!

#5–The Danger of a Dull Start

Often speakers spend so much time in setting up the backstory or reason why they are talking on the subject of choice, that they lose the audience before they ever get to the meat of the message. Start with a big hook to grab their attention.

The beginning of your speech is when listeners decide if they will stay tuned and engaged, or if they will tune-out and let their mind surf daydreams.

#6–The Danger of Copying Others' Material

Recycling is good except when you recycle content originating from someone else! Avoid using stories and key concepts from others unless you credit them as the source. Give attribution for information you pull from books as well. There's nothing worse than trying to pass off material as your own and someone in the audience recognizes the source. Know this: whether someone else recognizes the information or not, God knows. You honor him when you keep your integrity regarding crediting your sources.

Even better is when you use your own creativity to come up with original ways to discuss evergreen topics. There may be no new thing under the sun, but there are new ways to share it. Be sure to package your concepts in a fresh way, because new takes on old subjects are way more interesting than leftovers.

Determine if you are at risk for any of these dangers and prevent them before they become a reality in your speaking business. If you are brave, consider asking your wisdom team if they see any dangers from this list surfacing in your ministry. Honest inventory prevents big falls (and fails) from ever happening.

YOU WANT ME TO SPEAK ON WHAT?

E vent planners often ask us to create a speaking program to match their catchy themes. They expect the near impossible—for us to come up with biblical, inspirational messages or retreats to fit their subjects. Why do event planners pick such topics? Usually it's because they can't wait to decorate with this theme, or it's centered on a specific game or skit. They select the topic based on their part of the event rather than considering the challenge it creates for our part. What can we do?

As Christ followers, first we pray. Outlandish topics tend to stir up a whirlwind of chaos in our minds, and because of that, sometimes we forget to pray first. We dive in to research, brainstorming ideas that are often quite a reach to fit the theme. If event planners have prayed over a theme and are at peace with their selection, when we pray we complete the triangle, with God at the peak. He will assist us in building the right program for this specific audience.

Let me use some examples of difficult themes from my speaking ministry to show what I mean.

Tribute to America

One of my favorite event hosts assigned me the difficult topic of *Tribute to America* for a three-session women's conference. The event was near a military base and it was a year or two after 9-11, so patriotism was in the forefront of everyone's minds.

What was the problem? I can speak for patriotic events with no problem, if they are looking for an uplifting, motivational speech. But this venue needed biblical lessons directed to women, designed to encourage them in their Christian walk. America isn't in the Bible, so that was my first challenge.

I ended up with these three programs: (1) Remember Our Heritage, (2) Remember Our Heroes, and (3) Remember Our Hope. Even though it took a great deal of study to come up with the right material for this audience, the outcome was better than I imagined. This program ended up being one of the most powerful events in which I participated. And it all started with an uncomfortable assignment that led me to my knees in prayer.

Mysterious Ways

A retreat planner was eager to come up with a mystery-themed weekend to go along with a murder mystery activity she wanted to do for entertainment. I was assigned *Mysterious Ways* and instructed to prepare two messages for this rugged retreat setting on a working ranch. Do you know how difficult it is to tackle the mysteries of God and make it appropriate for women in such a casual setting? The hardest part was not to go so deep that I lost any relevant application for my audience.

I did a word search for mystery in the Bible and came up with two programs and several points for each message. My session titles ended up being: (1) The Mystery of Godliness, and (2) The Mystery of the Wisdom of God. That was seventeen years ago, and today I would probably come up with catchier phrases for the same topics. The main takeaway from this example is if you are given a difficult topic, research Scripture and let the verses create the points for your message.

Angels with Tilted Halos

A women's conference selected *Angels with Tilted Halos* to go along with Precious Moments artwork for their décor. This was probably the most difficult event theme for me because humans are not angels, and I didn't want the foundation for my three sessions to be biblically inaccurate.

I asked God to show me how I could be true to his Word while also honoring my event planner's wishes. I thought of the typical angel/devil drama we see represented in entertainment. The angel stands on one shoulder whispering in the person's ear, advocating for what is good and right. The devil stands on the opposite shoulder tempting the person to make the wrong choices.

I started the conference by painting a word picture depicting the tug of war we all go through in the fight over good and evil, right and wrong. I told them I had a vivid imagination and as the angel and devil duked it out, the angel's halo took a hit. Hence, angels with tilted halos. My three sessions covered the tug-of-war scenarios we deal with as Christian women, and how to make sure we are victorious by applying biblical solutions to our dilemmas.

Whew! That was my most challenging assignment. It kept me on my toes to be accurate with Scripture, and I made sure the audience knew the illustration was merely a human way of understanding a spiritual concept.

Lessons Learned

What can you learn from these examples to help you with your own topic challenges?

1. Pray for God to guide you as you prepare your messages.

2. Brainstorm with your event planners to be sure you know your audience and their needs.

3. After you shudder over the event theme, dig in. Research key words. I use biblegateway.com for this purpose. And don't forget to also search your topic using an online search engine. You might find quotes from high profile

individuals, fresh insights, or supporting examples to flesh out your message.

4. Be true to God and the Word, true to yourself, and true to your audience. If you do that, you can't go wrong!

It's not the end of the world when a venue asks you to speak on a topic outside your existing portfolio. It will stretch your creativity, open your eyes to new possibilities, and help diversify your repertoire. Keep in mind you may have to adjust your usual honorarium requirements to allow extra time for putting together a new program. But in the end, you will have stories to tell—just like me.

HELP! I DON'T KNOW WHAT TO WEAR

You get invited to speak for an event and you're uncertain what to wear. So many questions run through your mind. Should I wear my go-to outfit or buy something new? What will everyone else be wearing? I don't want to have a fashion faux pas or wardrobe malfunction.

I have found it works best to wear a two-piece outfit, preferably with a jacket on top, because over-the-ear mics and lapel mics have control packs that usually clip to a waistband. Nothing worse than wearing a dress and then finding out you need to clip that pack to something!

Personally, I prefer wearing slacks with a cami and jacket, for several reasons (modesty, comfort, style for my body type, etc.). But I also respect the wishes of churches that prefer women in dresses/skirts and wear a jacket and skirt to their events rather than a pantsuit.

I usually ask the event planner what the attendees are wearing, and I wear "one step up" as we were all trained, without acting like I'm putting myself on a pedestal. Unless it's a cozy girlfriends-in-jeans type gathering, and then I'd still wear a snazzier top, just for fun. For male speakers, ask if it's business casual or suit-and-tie.

Also think about your venue. One time I thought I'd do the "one step up" rule. The gals were in casual pants so I wore dressy pantsuits, and the location was a working ranch. My heels were not appropriate for walking across fields laced with . . . well you use your imagination. I looked like I was walking through a landmine field!

Seven main "what to wear" rules:

1. Wear something that makes you feel comfortable, so it puts your audience at ease. There's nothing worse than watching speakers tug at their apparel or scratching itches.

2. Wear something that makes you feel special, so it puts you in a full-energy frame of mind. Jazzed and ready to deliver!

3. Wear something that makes you feel like you are the authority on the subject, so that your posture reflects your preparation and experience. This helps authenticate your message.

4. Wear something that reflects your brand. Often I wear an aqua or teal accent because that's the color of my logo. When I distribute my literature that logo is burned into their memory. It's also considered a neutral color because it works with both genders and fits with most people's coloring and personalities.

5. Wear something that is modest for the setting. If the stage is elevated, some dresses and skirts might reveal more than is appropriate. Another modesty tip is to wear tights or leggings with your skirts/dresses.

6. Wear something layered. This look works for almost every body type and also prepares you for a room that is too cold or too hot. A blazer or cardigan works well. Another layering option, if temperature isn't an issue, is a classic or sporty vest.

7. Wear something that fits the culture of your audience. Some parts of the country dress differently than other parts.

Different ages define "dressy" a variety of ways. Do your homework and ask ahead of time.

You Decide

- Will you play it safe or display your individuality? Some prefer to express their personality and their brand with flamboyant colors, animal prints, western-wear or other eye-opening apparel. Others prefer to play it safe with business attire.

- Do you have a feature of your body you want to downplay or one you want to accentuate to draw the eye away from what you might consider a flaw?

- How do you like to accessorize? Do you wear one big statement piece and then a few understated items, or do you like to wear half your jewelry box at once? Is your go-to accessory a favorite scarf or tie?

- Will you be trendy or classic? Are you drawn to a new fad and what to try it out? The style rule is to only wear one cutting-edge fashion statement at a time. You don't want your clothes to scream before you even open your mouth to speak!

Other Hints

- If you need a place to hang your battery pack or mic clip, you might want to try the name badge cord. Sometimes I even take my own lanyard so I'm prepared.

- You were chosen to be the speaker of this event for a reason. They want *you*. So in selecting your wardrobe, be true to *you*. The worst thing you can do is wear something that ends up making you feel like a phony. It can stifle your connection with the audience and suffocate your message. I know some speakers try to wear something to fit every personality type so they all will be drawn to her. That might work for you, but to be honest, I find all it manages to do is to dilute your style by trying to make you something you're not. Sure…

experiment with styling outside your comfort zone, but ultimately be sure to pick what fits *you*.

- If you want to look more approachable—the friend rather than the expert—you might want to try wearing dark trouser jeans along with something jazzy to dress up the denim. And don't forget how different footwear can change an outfit.

- Consider wearing a color that coordinates with the event's decorating theme. You will blend with their décor and photos will look sharp, too.

- Know your own tendency to be too hot or too cold, and plan ahead for if the meeting room will be stuffy or over-cooled.

And finally, don't forget that the dilemma about what to wear actually needs to start from the inside out. If your inner person is dressed in God-ness, the outside will reflect the message he has called you to project. It's not merely a matter of fashion, but a matter of your attire being one more way you're living out your faith.

HELP—
I BOMBED!

I coached our student pastor (*Blake) to help him polish his speaking skills. When he spoke to our congregation, I thought he did a great job for his age and level of experience. But after the "Amen," he told me he felt like he bombed. His message really wasn't as awful as he felt. Isn't that often the case? Many of us finish a speaking presentation with negative impressions of how we performed, rather than enjoying an excited adrenalin rush I call "the afterglow." (Or sometimes we have both at the same time!)

If you've ever felt like a message flopped, this section is for you. The main thing, right at the start, is to remind yourself that even if you think you could have done better on a presentation, that doesn't mean *you* are a failure. We all have aspects of our speaking upon which we can improve.

Something I appreciated about Blake—he was open for suggestions. I asked him what he struggled with. He brought up the following issues. I helped him with practical suggestions, and am sharing them here, in case they might benefit you as well.

Point of Confusion

Blake was concerned that he didn't emphasize his main points. Why is that important? You want to make sure your audience is able to track with you as you present your material in a logical way that has a beginning, middle and end. The main points act as landmarks along the way—something memorable. Your illustrations aren't important if they don't point back to the takeaway you want to deliver. It's essential that you nail the main points. Make them short enough that you can see them in your notes and so the listener can remember them. If your main point is a paragraph, no wonder it gets lost.

Sometimes it's hard to read your notes when you get on stage. Nerves or pure excitement can cause your vision to be fuzzy and your mind to be foggy. The angle of the podium or pulpit can make it difficult to see the notes. The lighting can be challenging. To prevent these issues, it's essential to know your notes well enough that you only need them as a prompt of what's next.

I looked over Blake's notes and saw quickly that he buried the main points. Each one of them was in bold font. That's good, right? And large enough to see quickly. So what did he do wrong? They were all the last statement of each page, and then he used the next page of notes to back up the point.

Main Points

Never put your main points at the bottom of your page. Why? There are several reasons. Adrenalin can often cause us to go to the next page prematurely. We want to hurry up and turn the page so we don't miss the next thing. Almost like turning a sheet of music for an accompanist before she visualizes her last few notes. Another reason it's easy to bury our points if they're at the bottom is because our vision is not as sharp when we look that far down. The lighting and angle of the podium or pulpit contributes to this. I counteract that problem by adding more space to my bottom margin.

There's no rule that says you have to run your notes all the way to the bottom margin. If you are ready to type your next main point, start on a new page. Be sure your main points are in the top half of the page so you don't miss them.

Smooth Transitions

Blake and I also discussed how to use segues and transitional statements better to help build toward the next point and join the points for better cohesiveness. This also helps you remember what is coming up next, so you don't miss a main point.

Another reason Blake felt he wasn't effective is because the audience had blank faces. He wasn't getting instant feedback through body language, so he assumed the worst. What to do when this happens? I suggested he have some extra stories and humor available, as an emergency go-to if the audience goes cold. These are in addition to the ones built in to the message—keep them separate so you can find them right away. I use a notebook divider so I can flip right to them.

Also, realize they may not be thinking what you assume (Blake's wife was soaking it all in, impressed by his message, and he thought she had "stink face.")

Another way to receive warm body language from your audience is to vary your volume between regular, loud, and soft. Do the same thing with pacing: regular, fast, and slow, with emphasis. Don't scald people by keeping your delivery style on high-gear the entire message. Add variety in *what* you share, too. If it's all research facts, Scripture and direct quotes from other people's writing, it's too intense to soak in. After making a heavy point, soften it by telling stories or humor. Otherwise, the message stays too high impact. Think of a musical piece. Often they are most effective when you have a variety of tempos and volumes.

Blake also said he felt disorganized—papers flew everywhere and he couldn't read his notes. Since he prefers to use full-page paper notes, I suggested he try a 3-ring binder to keep them all in order.

Your next message will work better if you ask yourself these questions as you prepare:

- Am I sharing from a place of passion, not merely facts?

- Can others get a glimpse of my heart?
- Do I give them an aha! moment?
- Am I offering a unique perspective? For Blake, he shared Hebrews 12 from the perspective of a runner (he has a national collegiate championship ring in track). This made the passage come to life. He customized it, using his own story.
- Am I well prepared? Even though Blake missed some of his points, he delivered a message with solid content.

Blake thought he flopped, but he gave us plenty to think about, and we connected with his heart-core passion. We all walked away feeling uplifted and challenged. That's more important than knowing if a speaker missed some of his notes.

*Name changed

I DIDN'T EXPECT THAT RESPONSE!

Have you ever spoken to a group and you weren't sure if your words were making the intended impact? As a speaker, I tend to be fueled by the reception I get from the audience, and I'm sure you do too.

Here are some typical positive audience responses, when reacting at the appropriate moments:

- Laugh or look amused
- Sad
- Contemplative
- Inspired
- Motivated

Probably the best positive response is when you can see they are having lightbulb moments. They've just heard something that caused them to view an insight in a whole new way. These insights inspire transformation.

But what are some of the negative audience responses we see as we speak? (And maybe these have only happened to me . . . surely they don't happen when *you're* speaking!)

- Bored
- Disengaged
- Asleep
- Disturbed
- Confused
- Skeptical
- Whispering
- Yawning
- Squirming
- Texting
- Taking a call
- Eyes glassed over
- Arms crossed

Sometimes their body language simply means they aren't feeling well. Don't take it personally. And sometimes when a person is squirming it's because of pain, not due to them being uncomfortable with your words. They're just plain ol' uncomfortable! Others cross their arms or squirm when they're cold.

We're All Different

I've learned not to assign a meaning to the way I read audience response by their body language. Different denominations, parts of the country, culture, and more can determine how demonstrative audiences are in response to what they're hearing from a speaker's presentation.

But sometimes, you can have the same denomination, same town and same cultural background and *still* not have the same response to the same message in two different places. Let me give you an example. In one town I presented the same program to two different groups coming from the same demographics. Based on their responses you would have thought I aced one presentation and bombed the other. But I was reassured later that the crowd where I didn't have positive response actually was blessed by the program. Not only did they enjoy it (they could have told their faces that!)

they also took the insights home to contemplate further as they prayed in their quiet time with God.

I share that so you know that sometimes you can do everything right and still not get the response you were going for. But that doesn't mean it's the end of the story. God will use your messages long after you finish the conclusion. (Reminds me of the Bible verse that says his Word will not return void. It will accomplish his purpose.) As speakers, we are planting seeds. Sometimes it takes good dirt, warm sunshine, and nourishing rain to produce the desired outcome. Other times, there is an immediate result. We have to be obedient to our part of the process and leave the harvest to God.

Evaluate what you could have done differently:

- If it appears you are losing the crowd, it's time to help them loosen up. Tell a heartwarming story, share something humorous that goes with the presentation, or get them involved by having them stand up and do something as a group. When I'm speaking an hour after lunch during a full-day event, I always plan for a "wake-up" jolt of some kind. And if in doubt, toss chocolate to the crowd!

- If you are speaking in a different denomination than your own and you notice them bristling at your message, it could be that you're using terminology they are unfamiliar with or define in different terms. Prevent it by making sure your notes work for that audience. And if you're too late for that, once you notice it happening, be aware of any church-ese terms for the rest of the presentation. Try to use everyday conversation words rather than "Sunday going to meeting" words.

- If the audience has experienced a tragedy in their community right before you arrived, it's possible your program is no longer suitable for what they need right then. Be prepared to change up your presentation to fit their situation. Be on the lookout for any signs indicating you need a change. (It's best to find this out before you arrive, but even after you start speaking, if you notice untoward body language, adjust your message. This is when we multi-task by praying to God seeking his wisdom while still talking to the audience!

- If you're assigned a long timeslot there's nothing wrong with delivering a shorter program than expected if you notice you're losing the audience. If it's a great deal less time than allotted, then figure out how to fill that extra time. Sometimes I've asked them to split up and go to different parts of the building or outdoors, to have some God-and-me alone time to contemplate. Some have said this was the best time of the whole event.

  Other times I've asked people to pair up with an assignment to get to know each other better. One time I had volunteers come up to act out an impromptu skit. You can also leave time at the end of your presentation for questions and answers. There are many ways you can fill a long timeslot without risking audience boredom or listening fatigue.

God shows up differently to work in unique ways in the lives of very different individuals. We can't compare one event to another even if it's the same presentation. Each group will respond in a variety of ways. It doesn't necessarily mean you are failing and flailing. But do use any perceived negative responses as a way to take the temperature of your audience and adjust on the fly, if needed. When you learn how to draw your audience in, you are a successful communicator.

WHILE YOU WAIT

A re you waiting on something before you're able to get to the next step as a communicator? Does it make you feel like you are stuck or your career is delayed?

I've heard many say they are waiting:

- To save up money for a new website.
- For someone to barter with them to design print materials.
- For that church member who does videos to offer to create your demo video clip.
- For event planners to call.
- For someone else to spread the word about them because they aren't self-promoters.
- For toastmasters to honor them with an award so they can be an "award-winning speaker."
- For speakers bureaus to find them events.
- To get invited to a paid speaking gig.
- For an organization to recruit them to be a spokesperson so they can go on the road as a speaker.

- For a literary agent to sign them➔ so they get book deals➔ so they have book tables➔ because that's when they have enough status to be invited to the bigger gigs.

Speakers are also waiting for:
- An empty nest.
- Their little ones to get older so they can leave them more.
- Their teens to get drivers licenses so they can become the family taxi.
- Their caregiving situations to change.
- Their spouse to make more money so they can do the writing/speaking thing full-time.
- Their life dramas to quiet down.

Waiting is a dangerous place to be. It whispers in your ear that it's okay to do nothing until something outside your control happens. It convinces you that you're stuck until that certain something happens. It lulls you into complacency and even causes bitterness to grow when that thing doesn't happen according to your timetable. Waiting tells you that you have permission to slack off. Or worse, sometimes it causes you to question if you are even supposed to be a communicator.

A Busy Waiter

If you want to be a busy speaker, you have to be a busy waiter. Get active, don't wait for life to happen to you. There's plenty within your control for you to work on while you wait. First, make sure you get your direction from God. Receive his assignment so you aren't simply spinning your wheels. Once you have determined your mission, your purpose, and your goals, then it's time to make a list and check it twice.

Ideas to implement during your "active waiting" period:

Learn a new skill. Rather than wait for someone else to help you, research how to do it yourself. You can learn virtually anything online. With your new knowledge you can create a blog or website, learn how to do an e-mailer, customize a PowerPoint for your speaking presentation, or design a meme. You can do this!

Make a mailing list. Input all the contact info into a spreadsheet to use for your next mailer, whether it's a print mailer or an e-blast. Contact people to get permission to add their names to the list and recruit new sign-ups.

Don't wait for the phone to ring to pick it up. After you send out a mailer, it's up to you to follow up. Almost no event planners I know call a speaker merely because they get a postcard, mailer, or e-blast of some kind (unless they know you). You'll have to do the next step and make some follow-up calls. I know this is the hard part, but it's the part that gets you bookings. And if it's too uncomfortable to self-promote (I know how awkward that is) you can trade with another speaker and make calls for each other.

Hire a booking agent. If your speaking schedule isn't as full as you'd like, do something about it. A good time to hire a booking agent is after you send out a mailer or e-blast. You can train a local person and pay him or her minimum wage plus a percentage of any honorarium negotiated. (If you don't have money to do this, consider what you can give up so you "make" money. Example: I've gone from salon hair color to do-it-yourself color and stretched my 4-week haircuts to 8 weeks. I gave up getting occasional pedicures and now only get one at the start of the summer season. By doing this over the course of half a year I saved enough for the next thing on my professional wish list.)

Know what to say when you follow up. Whether you make the calls, or someone makes them for you, be prepared. If you make your own calls, do not say, "Will you book me?" Instead, call and ask if they've seen the mailer, and see if they have any questions. Tell them why you're a speaker. Let them hear your heart. Discover what events they have in the next year and discuss how you can help them. Be like a matchmaker. Find out their need and then match up what program you think might best fit that need. And of course, if you sent the mailer to them on the recommendation of someone, mention that person you have in common.

Do Something

Don't allow yourself to get stuck in the wait. Make plans for this new speaker season in a new way. What is one project you can do to improve your speaking ministry/business? Pick what needs to be done next. Or what you've put off. Or what works into your schedule and budget. Pick *something* to propel your career forward. As the cliché goes, "Don't just sit there, do something."

MARKETING MINISTRY DILEMMA

The most important of all challenges when it comes to publicity is knowing how to promote the message God has given you without promoting yourself.

It goes against the grain of Christ followers who have freshly learned to live sacrificial lives of humility, to promote ourselves. It's almost as if we finally figured out how to deny self and now we are asked to promote self. It doesn't add up. Self-promotion is an age-old dilemma for Christians. It's important to study the biblical view of promotion and discover your call to spread the word through God's marketing plan so that you aren't sucked in to ego-feeding marketing techniques.

Ponder these questions to develop your own marketing philosophy:

- If ministry is supposed to be spiritual (the fruit of humility comes to mind), doesn't that conflict with marketing (all about self)?

- Are my marketing plans to promote self or promoting God's message?

- If I say I'm trusting God to provide opportunities, then why do I need to seek exposure by promoting my speaking ministry? Won't God always send the right amount of speaking gigs to fulfill his plan?

- Will marketing feed my pride? How do I combat that to make sure it doesn't happen?

Marketing Motives

As long as your ambition for speaking is a God-sparked desire and not a self-focused drive, then your motive is in the right place, and you will be able to market with godly intention. That will be reflected in your style of marketing and will result in as many speaking opportunities as is suitable for God's purpose in your life.

You will have seasons when the gigs dry up and you wonder why. As long as you are doing everything you can to get the word out, trust that God knows why he has closed doors for a while. Often in hindsight you'll be able to see why. Timing is everything! Perhaps there's an illness, a family need, a rush deadline for another project, or some other reason why God sidelined you from speaking. Or maybe God has a life lesson for you to learn that will equip and empower your speaking in a new way. Once you are past that learning season you will move into a booking season and have a brand-new message that came out of your dry time.

If God wants you to be a speaker, he will lead you to know what types of marketing approaches to try. In fact, ask God to be the head of your marketing department and you will be blown away by the results!

Imagine fifty years ago when revival services changed our churches and communities. Individuals sensed the power of God in those events. Those revival coordinators used every marketing method known at that time. Why should today be different? Use every modern promotional method possible, as long as it doesn't violate scriptural principles, to get the word out. If God is in it, then he wants you to tell others.

Invest in Your Calling

Often when Christians say God is going to give them this big speaking ministry, they expect God to do all the work. Throughout Scripture we see that God asks something of his speakers—they need to trust, they need to obey, and they need to step out. It's a matter of investing in the calling. Marketing is part of that investment of time and resources.

If God has gifted you with speaking ability, then it's wrong to hide it just like it's wrong to hide any other God-given gift. He wants us to not only operate in our strengths, but also make sure others know how these strengths might make a difference in their lives. It is good stewardship to invest in the gifts entrusted to us.

Note: This same information applies whether your message is for a general audience or a faith-based event. God leads Christians to speak in all different types of venues with different purposes and messages. Whether the message is filled with Scripture or not, the speaker who is a Christian can seek God's direction and use his principles for marketing.

Often, we can look at a person's marketing strategies and determine where they are on their faith walk. If the spotlight is pointed on the message, the individual has a good handle on promotion, but if the spotlight is directed at self, they have probably gotten caught up in the tempting web of self-adoration. Dangerous ground—and it can happen to any of us if we're not careful.

Ethical Marketing

Marketing involves many ethical choices—it's wise to use some of your planning time to develop a careful and cautious, yet charismatic perspective on promotion.

One Christian publicist described how he writes promotional materials for his clients. He said, "For my work as a freelance publicist, I have to spin media materials in a way that gets the attention of hosts, producers or editors." The word spin raises the hair on the back of my neck. Sounds a lot like manipulating degrees of truth and lies for the benefit of the client. This is one extreme in the industry—following after worldly techniques without concern for biblical ethics. The other extreme is just as dangerous.

An author quoted Proverbs 27:2 to me. "Let another praise you and not your own mouth, a stranger, and not your own lips." He used this verse to justify doing zero publicity, marketing or promotion for his speaking and writing career. He didn't merely feel uncomfortable in the spotlight—he felt it was sin. This extreme is adept at hiding light under a bushel.

What do you say to these extremes, and how do you set your own marketing goals? I've determined it's always wise to see how the Bible handles similar dilemmas. My biggest calling is to be like those who experienced Jesus and said, "Come and see." My clients are all believers and their messages are words God has given them. Our responsibility is to go out and say to the masses and the individuals, "Come and see." As I promote my own work, I use that same strategy. I'm not inviting them to come and see me—I'm inviting them to come and see the work God is doing. It's his message. No one glorifies the conduit that delivers the water. The spotlight is on the refreshing truths communicated as it spills or splashes out of the vessel.

Try on a different perspective about marketing—one that will help you as you tiptoe through the promotional landmines. Here it is: Anything God leads you to do, you are called to do with all your heart, soul, mind, and strength. You are to do heartily (with gusto), as if working for the Lord and not to please others (Colossians 3:23).

To practically promote your message, make sure you:

- Provide value-added material for the audience through your promotional materials. What's in it for them? Every piece of promo literature should give readers something extra.

- Elevate good words you read by others—even if they are your competitors. Not flattery, but true praise. Good and godly promotion includes cross-promotion of others. Oh how I love the word cross in that phrase! As a double meaning, it points to the very motive behind cross promotion—selflessness.

- Only say in print what you would dare to say in person. If you wouldn't stand around at a party bragging about your latest project ad nauseum, then avoid doing so in an e-blast.

- Relay how jazzed you are with the blessings of this project—giving God the glory for the open doors.

- Have pure motives. When the heart is right, the words can't go wrong because out of the mouth comes the intentions of the heart.

- Ask for God to lead the way and to put his hand of blessing on it according to his good purposes—not according to your agenda.

- Look for opportunities to go and tell others about the project rather than waiting for them to come and see.

GOD'S MARKETING PLAN

God works alongside us as we prepare our spoken and written messages. Our words aren't inspired the way the Bible was inspired, but as we allow God to guide our pens (or our keyboards), we produce God-led text. Do you think he wants us to sit on that text and not disperse it? No way. Not any more than he wants us to put the kibosh on the gospel message. Words have the power to change people. Words have the potential of empowering and equipping and educating and entertaining. Others won't know about our articles and books if we don't promote those projects, and they won't know about our ability to deliver the spoken word at events if we don't spread the word.

Focus on the message of good news. What's in it for the hearer/the reader? Your project, whether faith-based or a general topic, contains something of value or the Lord wouldn't have led you to it.

> *Jesus traveled through all the towns and villages of that area, teaching in the synagogues and announcing the Good News about the Kingdom.* (Matthew 9:35a)

> *And the Good News about the Kingdom will be preached*
> *throughout the whole world.* (Matthew 24:14a)

How shall they be "saved" unless they hear? Others

won't hear about your speaking ministry/ business (the one God led
you to build) unless you tell them.

> *But how can they call on him to save them unless they*
> *believe in him? And how can they believe in him if they*
> *have never heard about him? And how can they hear about*
> *him unless someone tells them?* (Romans 10:14)

Don't hide it under a bushel. Why would God lead you to

be a speaker, only for you to hide it? The goal of light is to shine.
No one knows your work like you do, so even if you have a team of
promoters, don't allow your light to dim by hiding it.

> *No one lights a lamp and then hides it or puts it under a*
> *basket. Instead, a lamp is placed on a stand, where its light*
> *can be seen by all who enter the house.* (Luke 11:33)

Don't bury it. Don't get so caught up in other projects that you

end up burying your speaker marketing efforts.

> *But the servant who received the one bag of silver dug a*
> *hole in the ground and hid the master's money.* (Matthew
> 25:18)

Jerusalem, Judea, Samaria, and to the ends of the

earth. A marketing plan needs to include: local, regional, statewide,
and national/international emphasis.

> *But you will receive power when the Holy Spirit comes upon*
> *you. And you will be my witnesses, telling people about me*
> *everywhere—in Jerusalem, throughout Judea, in Samaria,*
> *and to the ends of the earth.* (Acts 1:8)

Go into highways and byways and compel them to

come in. The word *compel* here means to forcefully urge—coerce.

Obviously, marketing techniques that annoy people will not be effective, but if a message is worth making, it's worth marketing!

Consider connecting with all categories of marketing targets: consumers, niche markets, retailers, media, groups and organizations, ministries, book reviewers, bloggers, social networks, influencers, endorsers, librarians, etc.

> *And the master said to the servant, "Go out to the highways and hedges and compel people to come in, that my house may be filled."* (Luke 14:23 ESV)

Go and tell. Make an effort to leave the house—if you're a writer who also speaks, this might be hard to do. Writers are often happiest at their computers, but we need to work our feet as well as our fingers!

> *And how will anyone go and tell them without being sent? That is why the Scriptures say, "How beautiful are the feet of messengers who bring good news!"* (Romans 10:15)

Shine the Light! What can you do to spotlight your message and not spotlight you?

> *In the same way, let your good deeds shine out for all to see, so that everyone will praise your heavenly Father.* (Matthew 5:16)

> *The light shines in the darkness, and the darkness can never extinguish it.* (John 1:5)

Be one of God's messengers. God has always dispatched angels and humans to spread the word. We are messengers through marketing and publicity, spreading the good news of the message he's given us to write, speak, and share.

View your work in the marketing project as being a spokesperson for God's project. This is not self-promoting; it's telling others about his work.

Each one reach one. This is, at the core, a simple ripple effect. What are some ways for you to create grassroots buzz and go viral? Read John 1:35-46 and you'll notice a theme. *Come and see!*

Cast your bread upon the water. Try more than one marketing technique. See what bread morsels float and what sinks. Don't put all your emphasis on mailers or media. Promotion is so much more!

> *Cast your bread upon the waters, for you will find it after many days.* (Ecclesiastes 11:1 ESV)

Don't cast pearls before swine. Be selective in determining the recipients of your promotional efforts. Don't waste your time on the wrong targets.

> *Don't waste what is holy on people who are unholy. Don't throw your pearls to pigs! They will trample the pearls, then turn and attack you.* (Matthew 7:6)

**Let someone else promote YOU.
You simply promote the message
and the GOD of the message.
That's the balance.**

SECTION FIVE

SPEAKING CHECKLISTS
Lining Up Your Resources

PHOTO SHOOT TIPS

After I posted photos from my personal photo shoot, I heard from authors and speakers, all with the same request. *Teach me how to have a successful photo shoot.* Communicators need headshots and lifestyle photos for many purposes. Your image is part of your brand.

Tips to Get Started

- Research photos you like of others ahead of time. This will help you know the kind of posing and backgrounds that resonate with you. Use these to decide if you want any special effects.

- Make sure you know your branding impression well enough to explain it to the photographer. Your biggest goal is for the photos to reveal the unique "it" factor God implanted in you.

- Get your hairstyle the way you want it in the months leading up to the shoot, so you know the week it looks best after a cut or chemical process.

Choosing a Photographer

- Read resume/bio
- Check out portfolio, looking for models most similar to you
- See if the photos enhance the subject (you), or focus more on creating artistic impressions from the background
- Ask prior clients if satisfied
- Get recommendations

Discuss What You Want

This might include:

- Head shots
- Personality shots
- Outdoor natural lighting, indoors, or in-studio
- Interesting backgrounds
- Props (a book, a podium, a mic, etc.)
- Special effects
- Photo editing
- Pose ideas
- Permission to use the photos for professional purposes (with photo credit)
- Web and print versions of the photos
- Captured essence—explain your branding impression

Also mention any concerns you might have. Tell the photographer features that cause you to be self-conscious, so they can highlight your strengths and minimize your flaws.

Prepare for the Photo Shoot

- Pray and speak positive biblical self-talk to flip the script on the whole "I have terrible photo shoots" mentality.

- Look over the photo location ahead of time to discover the choice spots and to determine the best time of day.

- Time the shoot for when your hair looks best after a visit to the salon or barber.

- Try on clothing options the week before the shoot. Take photos. If uncertain which choice is best, share photos with wardrobe-savvy friends and ask for advice. When doing this, be sure to also coordinate your accessories and wear in the test photos, to make sure they are the best options.

- Once you choose your garments, make sure they are pressed, have no strings hanging down, and are ready for your big day. Use a lint roller to pick up hair, specks, etc.

- Study poses online. Share the ones you like with your photographer ahead of time.

- Discuss locations and make sure you and your photographer are both happy with the site.

- Give the photographer your phone number and get theirs.

- Have a Plan B for inclement weather, if you have an outdoor site.

- Women, you might want to visit with a make-up consultant for tips prior to your big day. You don't have to purchase their products to get advice. Have a makeover to try new techniques.

- Consider inviting a friend to be your stylist at the shoot. They can make sure your collar is straight, your garments are smoothed out, no lint or strings are visible, no lipstick is on your teeth, and your hair is behaving.

- Rest. Destress. If you carry the weight of the world to the photo shoot with you, the camera will find it.

- Use special eye treatments ahead of time to reduce swelling, bags, or discoloration.

- Consider if you want to use teeth whitening products.

- Anticipate rather than dread the upcoming shoot.

The Day of the Shoot

- Style hair in a flattering style, taking extra care to make sure it will hold up against humidity or changing positions.

- If you're a female, spend more time with your make-up. Consider using contouring and highlighting methods. Keep the lighting in mind.

- Apply petroleum jelly to your teeth if you have an issue with dry mouth. This will help you grin without your lips catching on your teeth and will prevent lipstick staining your teeth.

- If you have a jacket, wait to put it on until it's time for the designated jacket shots. The photographer might want to take some photos without the jacket, and if you've worn it to the appointment, your shirt could be wrinkled.

- Arrive early to allow time to get comfortable in your surroundings. You don't want to bring stress into the photo shoot with you!

During the Shoot

- Ask for a variety of poses and backgrounds if possible. You'll never know which one works for you unless you try.

- Try different smiles or serious looks. Laugh often. Make sure the camera captures what you want the viewer to see about your heart.

- Look in different directions—not always straight at the camera.

What Not to Do

- Wear your make-up in a style that is trendy, but not "you." It's fine to enhance your natural look, but don't go too far from the way you look when you're on stage speaking.

- Try a new hairstyle for your photo shoot. It should be the one you have when you show up for events. (I like a variety of hairstyles, so I'm not saying you can't be different—just that it's realistic for how you look in real life.)

- Use photo edits to the point you are unrecognizable. You might think it looks better to smooth out all the wrinkles and take away some extra pounds but imagine the surprise of your audiences when you show up in person!

Different Types of Photos

- Web photos are low-resolution.

- Print photos are high-resolution.

- Headshots can be just the face, at a neat angle and lighting, or include the neck and collarbone area.

- Waist-up photo positions sometimes work well.

- Full-body shots are often used to show personality or to reveal more of the surrounding setting.

- Vertical and horizontal photos. Ask for both to use in different professional settings as requested by your designers/ editors.

- Off-center photo. Try taking a photo with you to one side of the shot, with enough blank room on the other side to include text when creating specialty images.

- Personality photos. Decide what type you need, to fit your style and brand.

When it's Time for a New Photo Shoot

- When you're ready to launch a new campaign and you've already used your prior photos in previous promotions.

- When your appearance has had a drastic change (weight, hair, glasses, etc.).

- When your branding impression changes.

- When your target market/audience changes.

- When your website is being updated (consider the colors used on your site).

Do you need a new photo shoot? If you're pondering this question, it's time.

HOW TO BUILD AND USE A MAILING LIST

Your mailing list works for newsletters as well as other promotional materials.

1. Invite people to sign up at speaking events, book signings, vendor table events.

2. Have a newsletter sign-up form on your website.

3. Include your link for newsletter sign-ups in your bio. Use your bio on any articles posted online, where it's easy for them to click over and sign up.

4. Post notices on your blog and social media sites, with links directed to the sign-up form.

5. Give incentives to sign up, such as drawings for giveaways, a free downloadable PDF or e-book, an audio or video message, etc. (Be sure to follow current laws.)

6. Exchange business cards at networking events and input the data. Make sure to contact them to invite them so you have each individual's consent.

7. Hang out where event planners, coordinators, women's ministry leaders, etc. spend time online. Interact with them— not to hit them up, but to build relationships. This is so important for many reasons. But one benefit is that eventually you will have an open door to ask them if you can add them to your mailing list for an upcoming mailer. Where might you find these groups? Facebook Groups, Linked-in Groups, etc.

8. Ask other professionals to mention you in their newsletters along with a link where they can sign up for your newsletter, OR offer to write a guest article for their newsletters, blogs, etc.

9. Cross-promote with similar speakers. Give them exposure to your scope of reach and see what they can do to give you exposure with their contacts. This way, you both grow your mailing lists.

10. Go to websites of similar speakers who live within 200 miles of you for a regional mailing list or nationwide if you are building a national mailing list. Look for their speaking calendars. Input the data into a spreadsheet (name of group, location, etc.). Then look up that organization or ministry and find the remaining information you need for your mailing list (contact person, e-mail address, etc.).

Personally contact each lead and see if they'd be interested in being added to your mailing list so they receive your next mailer. Let them know they can opt out at any time. Then, the next time you send out a speaker promo mailing, your information will land in the hands of new contacts who will have future events requiring speakers like you.

E-blast Servers

- Aweber
- iContact
- MailChimp

- Constant Contact
- MyEmma

Be aware of laws related to the CAN-SPAM Act and GDPR (General Data Protection Regulation) and develop a strategy based on your own business ethics and preferences.

BEFORE STARTING A NEWSLETTER

There is so much that goes into doing a newsletter well. I recommend doing some deep soul-searching, prioritizing, and planning before undertaking such a task. These questions will help you as you plan.

1. What is your goal for starting a newsletter?

2. Who is your intended audience? How will you get names/ contact info?

3. Do you plan to send it via e-mail, e-blast, or snail mail?

4. Will it be set up like a letter, or more like a short collection of different articles?

5. To save space, will you be setting up links to the full articles rather than including the full text?

6. How will you infuse your newsletter with your brand? Will you have a logo?

7. What sort of value-added resources will you provide in your newsletter?

8. Will you offer incentives for people signing up for your mailing list?

9. Will you use a familiar color combination and page layout each time so the consistent feel of the letter helps your readers navigate your mailer?

10. How often do you want to send out your newsletter? Make sure this is part of the newsletter description, along with giving details of the content they can expect to receive if they sign up.

11. Will you collect sign-ups at speaking events?

12. What elements will you include? Some include their speaker/ professional calendar, advice, recipes, letters from readers, endorsements, a personal note, links to articles online, news updates, book release information, prayer requests, a welcome to new readers who sign up after certain speaking events, bullet points, Top Ten Lists, pull quotes, etc.

13. Will it contain your contact information and your social media links?

14. Will you have share links to social media?

15. Do you have a blog? If so, will it include a link to that as well as to your website?

16. What photos will you use? Find legal sources for photos you download or use your own photography.

EVALUATE YOUR SPEAKER PROMO KIT

For Print and E-blast Materials

- Do you have quality photos (usually an odd number: 1, 3 or 5)?

- Do you use a logo and if so, does it go well with your branding?

- Is your branding impression or tagline information clear?

- Do you give at least two ways for interested parties to contact you?

- Do you give specific program titles and descriptive blurbs? Do the blurbs sell your presentations?

- If you sing, is this mentioned in the promo kit?

- Do you spotlight quality endorsements from others?

- Is your color scheme and graphic style eye-catching? Does it match your style and branding? Will it grab the attention of your niche-audiences?

- Does your bio capture your essence and sell you?

- Do you include your social media links?

- What is your print format for this speaker promo? a) 2-sided glossy one-sheet, b) tri-fold brochure, or c) business envelope-sized rack card
- Does it mention products you have available? Books, CDs, DVDs, etc.?

Optional Items to Include in Your Speaker Promo Kit

- Speaker contract or agreement
- Endorsement sheet
- Deposit/honorarium information
- DVD or CD of sample program or clips
- Media and promo kit for event planner to use to promote booked event
- Event kit (fully planned to-do list and resources to give them a turnkey event)
- Additional resources

SUGGESTED SPEAKER FEE RATES

The following speaker fee schedule helps you determine which category best fits your status, and what your speaker fee range might be for this level of exposure and experience. The low end of the fee range is the usual fee for a single event, and the high end is for multiple speaking programs at one event (such as a retreat or conference).

High Profile—National: Do you have a high profile nationally? This includes a great deal of name recognition and probably multiple books you have authored. Consumers are familiar with your brand or platform. Do you have a national radio show or syndicated show or get featured often as a guest on national TV and radio? Do you have a social media reach of at least 30,000 contacts? **Speaking Fee:** $1,000-$10,000+

High Profile—Regional: Do you have some name recognition nationally, especially in your niche? Are you invited to share the speaking platform with high-profile speakers? Do you have some books published or have a fairly recognizable brand or platform? Do you have a regional radio show or get featured often as a guest on local radio and TV? Do you have a social media reach of at least 15,000? **Speaking Fee:** $500-$5,000

Niche Profile: Do you have name recognition in specific circles? Are certain groups, denominations or regions familiar with your name? Have you published at least one book or have a national column? Do you have a local radio show? Do you have a social media reach of at least 5,000? **Speaking Fee:** $400-$2,500

Intermediate Profile: Have you developed your platform and branding, and some small speaking and writing credits to your name? Do you have a social media reach of at least 2,500 contacts? **Speaking Fee:** $100-$1,000

Introductory Profile: Do you want to break into the writing and speaking industry, but are just starting out? Do you have a social media account? **Speaking Fee:** $0-$600

EVENT PLANNER WISH LIST

If your event planner could have a conversation with you, he or she might share something like this:

- **Prompt communication.** If I send you an e-mail, reply within a reasonable amount of time. If you cannot, at least send a quick e-mail to confirm receipt of my note and indicate when I can expect an answer from you. If I leave a voicemail, call me back within 24 hours if at all possible.

- **Authenticity.** Be real, not fake.

- **Humility.** I'm not drawn to divas. Be easy to work with—have no demands or unreasonable expectations. Be kind.

- **Professionalism.** Enough said.

- **No guesswork.** Be clear in your contract, your communication, and your printed materials. I don't want to have to work to read between the lines or wonder what you mean when you say something. Also, by providing most of the information I need online, I can quickly find answers to my general questions without having to bother you.

- **Integrity.** If something in our dealings causes me not to trust you or respect your work ethic, I can't build you up as I promote the event.

- **Life graduate.** It's so important to have more than book knowledge. Life experience qualifies a speaker better than someone who has studied hard, although both are important.

- **Alert to ministry opportunities.** Don't be so glued to your agenda that you miss an opportunity to reach out to someone who is hurting or seeking God.

- **Riveting.** I want my audience to be drawn in to your presentation and leave feeling glad to have attended the event. How will you dazzle the audience, while being true to your personality and style, and more importantly, true to your Lord?

- **Honor time limits.** This goes along with being flexible.

- **Aware of audience.** Know the season of life the majority of our audience is in—their biggest concerns and struggles, their goals, and how to best minister to them. This might affect your humor, your illustrations, your music and more.

- **Teacher.** Keep in mind that different members of the audience learn in different ways. Implement several learning styles into your presentation.

- **Humorous delivery.** Even if the subject matter is serious, there's usually an opportunity to add some lighthearted moments to the program without disrespecting the content. Humor is like loosening your belt an extra notch after over-eating—it allows space for all the good material the audience has consumed during the program.

- **Flexibility.** This means you don't have to have your way when it comes to decorations, program, time allotted to your sessions, or any other part of the event. You're simply there to serve. With that motive in mind, you'll be much more flexible.

- **Restraint.** It's difficult to listen to a speaker who is guilty of information-dump. All this achieves is brain overload. It's always better to hold back and leave us wanting more than to saturate us with too many points.

- **Reliability.** Be responsible. Once you accept a deposit and sign a speaking contract, don't back out if you get what you consider a bigger or better offer elsewhere. Plan to be timely when communicating your preparation for the event so I have peace of mind you will be early for the actual event too. There's nothing worse than panicking the speaker might be late!

- **Make me look good.** I don't go about being in the spotlight, and often work hard behind the scenes, but when the special speaker recognizes my hard work, it makes me feel good. And when the speaker is sharp—that also makes me look good!

- **Return on investment.** I want the event to be such a success that I can plan the next event, knowing the word of mouth will build on the success of this event.

QUESTIONS EVENT PLANNERS ASK

1. Is the speaker doctrinally sound?

2. Is the speaker an expert in his or her field?

3. What are the speaker's fees?

4. Will the speaker be funny or serious?

5. Will the speaker be professional, or will I be embarrassed by them?

6. Will the audience relate to the speaker?

7. Will the speaker be relevant?

8. Is the speaker willing to customize a program to fit our event?

9. Will the speaker interact with our group, or stay apart from the fellowship?

10. Will we feel like we've received even more than we anticipated, or will the program fall short of our expectations?

Final note from event planners: If you are particularly difficult to work with, not only will I refuse to book you for future events, but you will develop a reputation which will keep you from getting events with other groups. Avoid leaving a bad taste!

SPEAKER CONTRACT EXAMPLE

We covered what to include in a speaker contract (or agreement) in previous sections. Since it often helps to see an example, I created a dummy agreement for you. As you look over the following contract sample, decide what you need to include in your own. This is merely a mock-up, to help you envision your own.

Using a formal agreement of some kind is not only for legal purposes—it helps make sure both parties have the same understanding of what is being requested/offered. When you have several engagements on your schedule, it's easy to get them confused if you don't have these contracts to keep all the details straight. And I've been able to point to my contract when an event planner requests something different after the negation is complete.

AGREEMENT OF TERMS

Please sign both copies and return one with deposit.

Sponsor: _____

Organization: _____

Mailing Address: _____

City: _____ State: _____ Zip: _____

E-mail Address: _____

Phone: _____ Fax: _____

Speaker: _____

Name of Event: _____

Date of Engagement: _____ Time: _____

No. of Presentations: _____ No. of Attendees Expected: _____

Event Location: _____

Please contact _____to discuss topics and specific details of the event.

Financial Arrangements

Speaking Fee _____

Deposit of _____ is due by _____ to confirm the event.
   Make deposit check payable to: _____

Balance of _____ is due immediately following the event.
   Make check payable to the Speaker.

Transportation, Meals, Lodging *(Describe agreed-upon arrangement.)* _____

Travel Expenses *(Describe agreed-upon arrangement for reimbursement of travel expenses.)* _____

Additional Requirements and Information: *(List any extra wishes. Example: Lapel mic is preferred when possible. Please provide table and an assistant for the display and sale of Speaker's books, CDs and other resources. The Speaker will call for verification prior to shipping resources.)* _____

Cancellation Policy: Deposit is non-refundable. If event is cancelled by sponsor more than 90 days prior to the event date, no additional fees will be charged; if event is cancelled within 90 days of event date, 50% of the fee balance plus any event-related expenses the Speaker has already incurred are payable to the Speaker within thirty days of cancellation date.

We acknowldge and confirm that we have read and approve of the terms and conditions set forth in this agreement.

Sponsor _____   Speaker _____

Title _____   Date _____

Date _____

MEDIA KIT
WORKSHEET

When I worked on the newspaper staff, we received press releases all day long. They came via fax, e-mail, snail mail—even hand delivery. With limited staff on limited time, I confess we didn't give every release our full-fledged attention. They had to grab us and had to be relevant and current to garner our follow-up.

Knowing that history of most media rooms, don't you want to make sure your press release will at least get read?

Here are a few tips:

- In the opening paragraph tie your release to something that is currently in the news (a water cooler topic).
- Make the press release timely by connecting the theme to an upcoming holiday or awareness day/week/month.
- Quote a celebrity, and then segue to your announcement.
- Give the release local appeal—are you a high school alumnus, will you be speaking at a local event, etc.?
- Don't bury your hook in a subsequent paragraph—the most eye-catching material needs to be at the beginning.

- Come up with a catchy headline to introduce your press release concept.
  - Use action verbs.
  - Avoid adjectives and adverbs.
  - Remove unnecessary words such as: the, an, that.
  - Avoid punctuation in headlines—especially exclamation points.
  - If your headline is vague but quippy—fill in the blanks with a short subhead if you wish.

Imagine the headline and hook paragraph as a key. A key is small, but it's the only tool that will effectively open a locked door.

Once you have the headline and hook paragraph, fill in with other essentials. Make sure you have the basic journalistic who, what, when, where, why, and how. Provide an endorsement quote if possible so the release has clout. It's always better to have praise for your project in the words of someone else.

What to Avoid in Press Releases

- Spin
- Hype
- Sales pitches
- Overused terms such as announce, sought-after, etc.
- Sounding like an infomercial, with terms like best ever, one-of-a-kind, and others. If it sings like a commercial, they'll anticipate "but wait, there's more"—and not in a good way!

Format of Press Release

1. For Immediate Release
2. Contact Information
3. Headline
4. Dateline (date of the release and the originating city)
5. Opening Paragraph (the hook)
6. The Body of the Release (essentials only, or a specific angle)
7. Endorsement Quote
8. Bio and Press Photo

9. Book Cover Photo and sales information—if applicable (ISBN, retail price, publishing house, title, author name, release date, Web address to purchase book)

Media Kit (2-3 Pages)

1. **Press Release.** Try to get the actual press release on one page. Mention that you are now scheduling interviews. If you have content that works as a stand-alone article without an interview, you can give permission for the article to run as is in their publications. Ideally, the content should be about 400 words or less. If you are tight on space for the press release page, you can always wait to put the bio on the interview sheet.

2. **Endorsement Page.** Designate just one page for endorsements. Shorten long endorsements so they will more likely be read. Also play with the spacing and font size to give it the best look. If you have more endorsements than can fit on one page, consider adding: "more endorsements on website."

3. **Interview Sheet.** Provide six to ten interview questions they might ask. These should be questions that allow you to answer with engaging stories, and value-added content for the listener (entertain, inspire, inform, motivate, etc.). I put the press photo and bio on the interview sheet, even if it's on another page of the media kit, so the host feels a connection during the actual interview. Sometimes the interview sheet gets handed to the host, and the producer keeps the rest of the media kit—or pages get separated. By putting it all on one page, the host has everything he needs to introduce you to his listening audience and interview you—even if he hasn't researched your work or read your book.

Save your media kit as a PDF and offer as a download on your website. Make it easy to access, easy to search, and easy to find.

WRITE A SMART INTERVIEW SHEET

Media kits often contain interview sheets, also called tip sheets. How to write them? Work backwards. Think of your five to ten most important talking points and write questions that will enable you to give these answers during the interview. Discuss true-life illustrations. Audiences are engaged when hearing stories more than a string of facts. If you want facts to be mentioned, have the host give the fact as the lead-in to a question. That way you don't even have the risk of misquoting a statistic or fact.

Some interview sheets have two to four different interview angles, and under each of those will be three to four questions that tie in to that theme.

Interview angles can come from:

- Your area of expertise
- Your hobbies and passions
- Special holidays or awareness days/weeks/months, seasons or calendar days
- Water cooler topics—current news issues
- Evergreen topics—subjects always of interest to the public

Make sure you don't over-mention the book title or state "in the book" in the interview questions or your answers. This makes it sound too much like a sales pitch. Your host is looking to have a congenial conversation with you rather than produce an infomercial.

Be prepared for the host to go off script and ask you questions not found on your sheet. If they read your book or researched your work, they may highlight a concept you write about that will appeal to their audience. This interview sheet is merely a list of suggestions to help hosts who don't research ahead of time. It also helps them envision how an interview with you might shape up because they can understand the thread of conversation by reading your interview ideas. If they read the sheet and get a positive taste for how the interview might go, they are more likely to book you for an interview.

Your interview sheet should only contain the possible interview questions—not your answers. The actual interview will seem much more spontaneous and conversational if you don't have the answers typed word-for-word. It keeps the host guessing what you might say next and keeps you on your toes as well!

INTERVIEW CONFIRMATION FORM

Create an interview confirmation form so you don't get bookings confused—and so all the information is at the host's or producer's fingertips. I've heard of guests who missed interviews due to wrong date, time, time zone, contact information, knowing who is initiating the call, etc. Because of their nightmares, I formed an interview confirmation sheet. Keep a template ready and fill it in when you get an interview booking with media. Then send to all parties involved to keep mishaps to a minimum.

Include:

- Stationery Header (logo and contact info)
- Interview Date
- Interview Time and Time Zone
- Station and/or Show
- About the Program (this helps the one being interviewed prepare for the show by knowing that show's focus and audience)
- Host Name and Contact Info
- Booking Agent (Producer) Name and Contact Info

- Guest Name and Contact Info (be sure to have phone number and e-mail address—both!)
- Who Initiates the Call? What Number?
- Duration of Interview
- Topic of Interview
- Status of Mailed/E-mailed Info (book, media kit, any give-aways, etc.)

Also leave a column on your spreadsheet for other notes. You might want to know if the show is streamed live online or archived online, so you can promote it to your circle of influence. Hosts love it when you are willing to help them get the word out. You also might like to note if the show has given you permission to use the MP3 or video for your own promotional purposes, or if they prefer you link to their site.

EFFECTIVE RADIO

For radio exposure to work, first check your motives. When many of us started in the industry, one of our goals was to find a way to get on radio for ministry opportunities. We didn't want to sponsor our own segments, due to money limitations, but we felt God leading us to share the message he placed on our hearts to a bigger circle of listeners than our local group (church, organization, etc.).

You're the Expert

Before you set yourself up as a radio guest, you must seriously evaluate whether you have an engaging radio presence. Not everyone is gifted for radio. Don't force it to happen if it's not your thing.

Where to appear on radio and television? Pay attention when other speakers say they are being interviewed. Harvest the contact information, create a media mailing list, and promote yourself to these same outlets.

Radio helps legitimize you as an expert in your field. If you cringe at the word *expert*, substitute the word *passionate* and you'll feel more comfortable. What are your passion topics? These are your areas of expertise. If you deliver the goods, audiences will warm up to you and you will grow your tribe—your circle of influence—your reach. You are broadening platform, imprinting your brand, and all the other good things that help establish your career.

Becoming an expert on something gives us the avenue to be booked on radio. Now we have the opportunity to share the heart-core message God has given us. But by the time some speakers make it to radio, their motives and priorities have changed. They only care about book sales and speaking bookings. Sadly—it shows.

Not About Selling Books

Listeners can sense when guests are on media to sell books, or if their motive is to deliver a value-added segment that helps the audience. Avoid stilted answers that sound rehearsed. Teasers are off-putting, and force listeners to buy the book to learn more, rather than giving them information to use. Listeners end up switching the channel before the interview is over, and they certainly don't buy the book.

If your main goal for radio is to sell books, you will probably be disappointed. But if your main goal is to expose your message to new audiences, then you've found your niche—you can make a difference in the lives of others by making yourself available to media. Have in mind the reason why you are giving interviews. If you are grateful to get to engage an audience you would never get to meet otherwise, and you are there to help or entertain them, rather than to promote your projects, you will end up winning in the end. If listeners relate to what you are saying, that connection will help you develop your scope of reach for your ongoing platform.

Lagniappe. Giving your audience something extra. It's not just a teaser or marketing ploy.

MEDIA TRAINING

L earn how to be a grace-filled guest—it's your time to shine.

Extra media training will help:

- Increase name recognition.
- See more listeners convert to consumers of your products.
- Establish yourself as the go-to person of your brand—your passion.

Calm your nerves. Temper your expectations. Let your light shine as you answer interview questions on the radio or television. Use every interview opportunity to provide valuable information for your listening audience, and before you know it, you'll be a pro. They wouldn't think of changing the channel!

Interview opportunities help to brand you and promote your current projects. Consider asking for professional help in training for interviews with media. This includes: radio (either in-studio or by phone), television (live or taped), print publications, and internet. This section will help you get a head start on media training. By following these tips, you will engage with your host and audience, and will accomplish the goals set in place from this exposure.

At the Interview

- Watch casual remarks. Keep in mind that nothing is really off the record, and anything you say may end up permanently in print.

- Answer every question. "No comment" is never an acceptable answer. Avoid certain issues by transitioning to other topics. Use bridges to steer the conversation in order to deflect sticky questions, or to get to the meat of your message. One example of bridging is, "That's a good question. I haven't really thought about that. But one thing that I have been thinking about lately is . . . "

- Flag key points. When you're speaking, use flags to signal key points. Let the reporter know you are about to make a main point by using an indicator phrase such as, "the key point is . . . " or "the important thing to remember is . . . "

- Be interesting. If you are passionate about your subject, it will make a better impression.

Appearance (for TV)

- Women, bring your own makeup in case no makeup artist is available at the studio. If no artist is available, touch up your eyes and give yourself more color. Wear lip color to accent your grin and your words.

- Even when they say a makeup artist is available, be prepared to do your own makeup if the hosts are late and the artist is tied up doing their makeup until airtime.

- Be rested and avoid puffy eyes by using a cool compress across your eyes before applying makeup. This will give you a refreshed look for those early morning interviews. Or, if you know your skin is agreeable to the product, try hemorrhoid cream to shrink the delicate tissues of puffy eyes.

- Get someone with fashion sense to advise you. The visuals are all-important on TV. Dress like you mean it, and match the mood of your message. Consider your branding to select the appropriate image. Keep in mind that the person interviewing you will most likely be wearing a smart suit and will have had a recent haircut.

Body Language and Positioning

- During a television interview, when you are not actually speaking, always keep a pleasant look on your face. You never know when the producers will switch to a shot of you.

- There will often be a monitor (a television screen placed somewhere off-camera that faces you and shows the on-air talent what's being broadcast). Don't look at it! If you are looking there and the producers switch to a shot of you at that moment, you will appear to be looking down and away from your host, as though you are distracted or not paying attention. Also, anyone watching the program who is familiar with television production will know you are looking at yourself.

- Don't stiffen up. Lean forward now and then while talking to the host. The audience is quickly bored by rigid conversation (talking heads).

- Speaking of heads, avoid the bobble-head look of vigorously nodding your head yes. It really accentuates double chins and stretched or wrinkled skin around the neck, and also looks unprofessional—like you are trying too hard or are too eager to connect with the host.

- To prepare for your TV interview, watch newscasters with the sound off to see how they talk. What you'll see may surprise you. They use a lot of body movements. Since many camera angles are from the shoulders up, that means all the interest normally provided by human motion has to be condensed to the head, shoulders, and perhaps hands. Don't go crazy; don't make yourself look foolish. But put a little more energy into your conversation than you normally might. As Marshall McLuhan observed, television is a cool medium. It craves heat—and it's up to you to provide it.

- Think about hosts you like and emulate their style. They are probably at ease, direct and affable. You too can pull off this winning combination.

Awkward Moments

- If you are debating someone, keep a pleasant look on your face. Even viewers who agree with your opponent will like you and take you seriously if you appear calm, reasonable, and pleasant.

- This isn't a game show requiring you to beat the others to the buzzer, so you have a moment to collect your thoughts before answering a question. Take it.

- If you don't understand a question, ask the interviewer to clarify.

- If you stumble or make a mistake, correct yourself immediately. You want to make the most of this opportunity. If the interview is being taped and you don't like an answer you gave, ask to start over. (Save do-overs for extreme circumstances though. Try your best to be a one-take wonder.)

Remember

- The importance of story—personal examples trump statistics.

- The hosts are human too—don't be intimidated by their fame.

- Be relevant.

- If you're at home on a phone interview, raise your eyebrows or stand on your tippy toes to project positive energy (but avoid being hyper like a terrier).

- Your talking points. (Plan ahead of time the main issues you want to cover.)

- Breathe in, breathe out—relax and enjoy the process.

- Be flexible to adapt to whatever they throw your way.

- Be available. Don't make it difficult for them to book you for their show.

- Have your project fresh in mind. If you are working on new projects it might mean going back and looking over your old research again to sound knowledgeable and passionate on the topic.

Do

- Use humor (but only sparingly). Improvisational humor is better than canned jokes.

- Smile—have fun. Being prepared and confident helps a lot.

- Focus on the host and not the camera (or crew).

- Know what you want to say, practice it, and then say it when the camera's rolling.

- Think in terms of eight-second sound bites. Have about five points to make and learn how to integrate them into the interview no matter the questions.

- Forget that you're talking to millions of people. Just speak to the interviewer naturally—in your normal tone and volume—as if he or she is a good friend.

- Stay calm. A TV studio is a hectic place, whether it's a local news station or The Today Show. Don't panic if the staff seems stressed and disorganized—that's just everyday life in television. Ignore the hubbub and take control.

- Be yourself. Try to relax and speak to the reporter in conversational language. Avoid using buzzwords specific to your industry or organization. The reporter or the audience might be unfamiliar with those terms and feel lost in the interview. Often a host will end an interview early if there's too much vague terminology or slick selling techniques.

Don't

- Over-think your responses or they will sound canned.

- Repeat the question, because it comes across as giving yourself time to fabricate the answer. Reword the question only as a last resort to buy time to think of the right answer.

- Take notes with you except to review briefly before the show.

- Answer questions that are either irrelevant to you or for which you do not know the answer. But be sure you don't say, "that's irrelevant" or "I don't know." Come up with a way to transition to something that will impact the audience without disrespecting the host's question.

- Argue with a reporter, especially when you are on-camera.

- Feel that you should fill empty space after you've given a response. If you are not prepared to elaborate—don't. Sometimes interviewers use the pregnant pause, hoping you will panic and blurt out something to fill the quiet space. Just sit there and smile and wait for the next question after you believe you've sufficiently answered the question. If the pause is awkward, then if all else fails, offer to fill it with an anecdote rather than an uncertain fact.

Bonus Tips

- Whether you're on TV or radio to promote yourself or something else, you're there to convey a specific message. When it's your turn to speak, make sure you get your point across.

- Avoid trailing off on a topic not directly related to the subject of the interview. Hosts with ADHD or who have not studied for the interview might get sidetracked if their minds stray.

- Watch the pace of your reply. Talk too fast and it will appear you think you have more material than time and you're trying to cram it all in. Too laid back and you don't appear passionate about the subject.

- Beware of being monotone. Allow your voice to naturally rise and fall in pitch, volume and tone.

- Enunciate. There's nothing worse than an audience misunderstanding because you didn't properly enunciate a word or phrase.

- Beware of the "s" and "p" sounds because they tend to hiss and pop with certain mics.

- Use this opportunity to speak directly to this unique audience. Your platform has opened doors with the media, so use it to reach new audiences rather than sounding like a promotional clip.

- Set up your phone so you don't get call waiting, which can interrupt the interview and mute the speaker for a split second each time it rings.

- Use a landline for phone interviews, to cut down on risk for cell phone static interference and disconnects. If you use a cell phone, make sure you have a strong signal, and stay put.

- Don't forget to ask for an MP3, CD or DVD of the interview to use for promotional purposes after the show. Ask for permission to post it to your site. Some prefer you link to their online archives and others will give you full permission to use as you wish. (You might have to pay a fee to use their materials.)

- Have talking points, but don't be obvious about them—you want to come across as a passionate expert on the topic, rather than a politician. Don't over-think your responses or they will sound canned.

- The same goes for mentioning your book—you want to mention it, but limit your phrases of, "Well, in the book..." "When you read the book, you'll find . . . " And the worst is, "I'm not going to answer that question. You'll have to get the book to find out!"

The final word on interview guesting is this: if your main goal is to connect your message to the audience, then God is going to use you in a mighty way. He honors your work when your motives are pure. And the great thing is when your motive is to shine *his* light, he takes care of those other loaves-and-fishes needs in your life, such as making sure you have speaking engagements, selling books, and getting exposure.

WORKING WITH PUBLICISTS AND AGENTS

If you decide to hire a professional to help represent you to ministries, event coordinators, media and/or publishers, here are tips to help you make the most of your working relationships:

- Don't expect your professional team to do all the work for you. You will always be your best representative—no one can duplicate your passion. But they can multiply your efforts, so work in partnership with them to achieve optimal exposure.

- Be sure you know the communication preferences of your team. What seems like a pressing matter might not qualify for contacting them outside of their normal work hours, so be courteous of their time. Make appointments for any non-urgent phone calls, and use brief e-mails for most contact, unless they request otherwise.

- Don't expect your team to read your mind—be specific in discussing dreams, needs, and deadlines. Ask questions to minimize misunderstandings. Be clear about your expectations and contact your rep any time you are disappointed so they have the opportunity to achieve the measurable goals you have set.

- Keep up with current trends and discuss how you might implement these with your team. They may give you a traditional campaign unless you request more unconventional methods of obtaining the level of exposure you want for your project.

- Provide your team with a list of buzzwords that fit your project so they can sprinkle these key thoughts in their pitches with others. Avoid worn out expressions and use descriptive words unique to your work. This helps with branding your platform.

- Ask your team what else you can do to complement their efforts. They love hearing this!

- Share your networking connections and mailing lists with your team so they can utilize them in promoting you.

- Make yourself available for brainstorming sessions, interviews, and other branding projects as proposed by your team. Not doing so will limit your exposure and diminish the potential of your campaign.

- Tell your team what your travel schedule is so they can cluster additional media and speaking events in these locations.

- Forward any ideas you find online and in e-newsletters to help them consider new ways to get the word out about your work. They might miss something you've discovered, so don't assume they're already aware of these ideas that cross your desk.

- Send thank you notes to anyone your team has set up to give exposure to your project, whether online, in print, or broadcast. This also goes for ministries and businesses. A grateful speaker is going to win more bookings than ungrateful speakers every time.

- Give your team current photos to use in your promotion. They might hesitate to tell you that your press photo is out-of-date, and it hinders their efforts if you don't appear fresh and relevant to their targets.

- Pay your invoices on time with any professionals who represent you. It's hard for them to be passionate in their efforts when they feel like they're doing it for free.

AFTER THE EVENT

How do you feel after you give a presentation? What goes through your mind? Are you jazzed, or drained? Does it take a while to fall asleep? How do you handle the aftermath of an event? Does it feel more like an afterglow or after-fizzle? Let's talk about it.

Recently a friend gave a brilliant presentation at a conference. She successfully sat up and ran the technology without assistance. The presentation was skillfully delivered, and she was able to speak from the heart, engaging her audience. Because of the opportunity, she connected with several who can help propel her writing and speaking career. She recognizes the positive outcomes, but yet, she's fighting the niggling thoughts of a perfectionist. Her mind torments her with what could have been done better.

She knows she's focusing on minor details in comparison to the major victories, yet those negatives threaten to ruin her positive experience. As she runs through the positive feedback, she disqualifies each response by listing what she could have done to improve the session. Because she values quality and a strong work ethic, she tries to do the best possible, and anything less than that gives her cause for pause.

Have you ever experienced the struggle of negativity and perfectionism that threatens to derail your celebration after an event? How do you handle it?

Give God Credit

Pamela Thrift Robinson asks herself questions to remind her of the good. "Did God lead me to this speaking time? Do I believe he spoke through me? Lastly, do I believe his Word never returns void? If I give God credit for *victories* but don't expect him to use what I believe are my inadequacies then it becomes about me not him. Giving all credit to him helps me to trust him more. When he is in it, it will bear fruit."

Countermoves

Robin Steinweg shares, "I wait until my emotions aren't quite as involved (and after a good sleep and some food), and then evaluate, asking God to give me his perspective. I'd love to discount 100% of the negative thoughts, but in order to improve, I need to look with sober judgement (Romans 12:3). I just had a cool reminder of this while listening to a book called *How Children Succeed.* One of the most important parts for children after chess games is going over the moves and countermoves to evaluate what might have been done differently. The countermoves might be compared to the audience response. After all that, I remind myself that the rearview mirror is smaller than the windshield. Got to look ahead more than behind."

7 Ways to Debrief

Here are a few of the ways I've dealt with similar struggles at different times in my speaking career.

Quiet prayer. I tell the negative stuff to hush up so I can have some quiet. In the quiet I ask God to tell me how he felt about the day. And I open myself up to be willing to accept a "Well done, faithful Kathy," from him. I allow God to be the one to tell me how to feel about the experience and what he wants me to learn from it to equip me for future programs.

Celebrate victories. I tell myself I will evaluate the day with an open mind *after* I celebrate each victory of the day. I list the successes one by one and thank God for them. Then I realize that anything I say to undermine those victories is like telling God, "Thank you, but no thank you."

Advise others. I think about what I would tell someone else who is explaining away their good day—then apply this advice to myself. I receive both the instruction and the atta-girls, just like I'd share with another speaker, to spur them on.

Evaluate negatives. I give myself thirty minutes to evaluate the day without feelings—just the facts. I spend time to make a plan for improving what could have been better. But then I circle back around and ask myself what the goals were for the day and evaluate the perceived outcomes. I realize that even though there was room for improvement, the goals were achieved. Or if they weren't achieved, I remind myself the world doesn't revolve around me, so any lack of achieving those goals isn't only because of my failures. Others involved could have had bad days, different goals, or whatever.

Bullet lists. I make bullet lists of: the good, the bad, the victories, the struggles, the ahas! Sometimes, seeing lists helps to ground me—to center my thoughts and feelings.

Make plans. I set my next goals, so I can move forward and not get bogged down. I think about how I will handle the presentation differently next time because of what I learned this time. Also, I start working toward those open doors and opportunities that came about because of this event. That helps fuel my passion again.

Keep track. I write down specific feedback I received or observed so I don't forget or minimize the good responses or results. As I do this, I recognize God's fingerprints all over the day. Then I can sit in wonder and enjoy the afterglow. The after-fizzle is gone!

AFTER THE EVENT CHECKLIST

1. Ask for endorsements from attendees and/or event team.
2. Ask event coordinators if they can give you names of other groups that might like a similar program.
3. Send thank-you notes to all who helped you or made the event a success.
4. Mention the event on your social media sites, in a way that shows you enjoyed connecting with the group, shows your passion for the topic, and piques interest from those reading about it to book you for other events. Don't forget to post photos (unless it's a private affair).

Self-Evaluation

- Did I feel prepared when I got on the stage? What could I do better next time to prepare?
- How could I improve in the actual presentation of the message?
- What surprised me?
- What new material came to me as I presented the talk that I need to add to my notes for next time?

- What was the best part of having this opportunity?
- How did the PowerPoint or other visuals go?
- What key points seemed to especially hit home with the audience? Did any points fall flat? What can I do to fix that for the next time?
- Did I have any distractions or interruptions, and if so, how did I deal with them?
- Did anyone offer feedback?

SECTION SIX

SPEAKING CONUNDRUMS

Answering Questions

ANSWERING YOUR QUESTIONS

Recently I surveyed speakers, to find out what pressing needs they had in developing their speaking business. They gave me some great questions that represent the struggles of many speakers.

Add-on Requests

How do you recommend I handle add-on requests from event planners? Sometimes, they ask questions that the event planning team should do without the keynote speaker (me) being involved. Other requests could zap my speaking energy if I'm not careful. Examples: Could you meet with our planning team to help us with the details of the event? Would you help us with planning centerpiece ideas? Would you be able to put together a skit? What do you think we should serve? Could you also lead our worship time? Would you be able to teach one of our craft breakout classes at the event?

My answer depends on many factors. I offer to do turnkey events for some hosts, providing much of what you mentioned in your question, but they pay for my additional services. I enjoy doing them—having been an event planner for over 35 years. But if all you want to do is speak, then let them know you provide the speaking part of the program, but you aren't available to do anything extra.

Even if you are capable of doing those other things, that doesn't mean you've offered to do them, nor should they be expected. Only you can determine what you can provide for their event. Those other services would cost you in time and effort, so they should cost them, too.

Let the host team know what you will and will not offer. If they need a planning meeting with you prior to the event for more than your usual allotment of time, advise them of your hourly consulting rate or inform them that your other work won't allow extra time for that. Make sure they know they need to take care of the other details without you or contact a different speaker who provides turn-key events.

Reactions to My Fee

How should I respond to reactions regarding my speaking fee? It's modest and not at all close to what many speakers charge. I'm looking for specific grace-filled responses to this type of statement: "We really wish we could have you come, but we are a mission, and it isn't going to work." The church would have easily had the budget for the price break I offered because I know their budget. They called another speaker friend of mine and got sticker shock regarding her fee. What are some ways we can respond to the implication that if we get paid a fair wage that our ministry isn't really ministry?

I find a short non-defensive answer works best. Some hosts truly do not realize professional speakers earn a professional wage. With this type of host, you can educate them on what the going rate is for your level of skill, training, and experience.

Unfortunately, some hosts try to shame Christian speakers into feeling guilty for requesting an honorarium or fee, implying (or outright saying) it's unchristian to earn a living from ministry. It's their form of bargaining, or possibly even manipulating. I'm not sure you'd want to speak for this type of host, anyway.

I have different responses for different scenarios. Often it works to simply state you are a professional who invests a great deal of time in their event to make it top notch. Let them know it is ministry because you plan to minister to their leadership team as well as the attendees. Because of your ministry heart your rate is greatly reduced, considering your level of training and experience. Tell them what the going rate is, so they can learn that your rate truly is reasonable for what you offer.

If they continue to resist, you can mention that no other professional with a Christian worldview is asked to reduce their rates simply because they are believers. We pay our doctors, plumbers and store owners whatever their rates are—speakers should be no different. It's not a haggling arrangement. They are welcome to book a speaker with less experience and training who may have a lower fee.

Let's also address discussing our fees with potential event planners. I have different ways to approach it, depending on the circumstance and also depending on how God leads. If I'm already going to be in an area for another event, I have the ability to accept a love offering or reduced fee, to try to work within the group's budget. But if a group contacts me, and I need to travel to their event, working it into my schedule and coming up with a new message, I tell them what my usual honorarium is. If I don't have as much work involved (less travel, a message I already have developed, etc.) I might start the negotiation by asking what their budget is.

Technology Malfunctions

How should I prepare for technology malfunctions during speaking events or leading Bible studies? Example: The video or PowerPoint won't play.

The main way to prepare is to assume you will have zero technology and be ready in case that happens. By not dreading it, you won't break under pressure if it occurs. I've found God often works mightily when we have to go with Plan B. Even if you have to take a moment to regroup and ask someone to pray while you seek God's wisdom for your next course of action, that's okay.

Sometimes it's better to suggest the group take a ten-minute break so you can come up with a way to continue. I've even had to do this when there's no electricity (that's pretty basic technology that we tend to take for granted)! If you are *live* online and can't stop, then give yourself the same grace you'd give someone else in the same scenario, admit the hiccup to the group, and ask them to pray as you try to carry on. This happens to me often as I present webinars. I've learned to remove the pressure of expecting perfection, and this helps when technology fails to cooperate. And finally, remind yourself it isn't the end of the world. And if it is, our job is finished!

Clustered Events

You have mentioned clustered events. How do you arrange these?

I make sure my first booking is enough to pay the travel (or honorarium plus travel, depending on the budget). I build around that date with other gigs. I contact people I know in the area and ask them to help me get the word out. I also post on social media, mentioning where I'll be and ask for leads to bookings.

I offer to waive my usual honorarium and come for their regular budget since I'm already going to be there. This allows me to minister to some groups who might otherwise not be able to afford to bring me (or any speaker) in from out of state. Once I get to an area outside my home base, I want to be used as much as possible, so I schedule events back-to-back. There will be time for resting once I return home!

Follow-up

What is the proper follow-up with the event planner/host?

Before the event, talk through a speaking contract with her/him, so there are no surprises. A contract isn't merely to nail down the honorarium, but also to discuss time, location, lodging, transportation, microphone, stage set-up, technology, break-out sessions, handouts or other print needs, book table, etc.

After the event, send a thank-you and comment on a specific blessing from their event. Suggest future programs and ask if the event planner knows someone else who might like to schedule you.

Also, if they seemed pleased, ask for an endorsement blurb to use in your promotional materials.

Gifts

Do you recommend I give gifts to the audience? Should I give gifts to my hosts? (I feel like I should give gifts, but that gets expensive.)

If you have a product table, it's smart to give gifts from it during the program. This gesture honors the hosts and guests, and also raises awareness of your products. Gifts allow you to invest back into their ministry or organization.

If an overnight host provided lodging, it's nice to place a note on your bed—you might consider leaving a small gift, too. To keep expenses down, find an inexpensive gift that ties in to your brand or your program message. Notepads with a pen, a custom magnet with a core message from your work, or a product from your table.

I buy potential gifts in bulk when I see them on sale or clearance. Besides magnets and note pads, I buy: bath products (with a name or color that fits with the product table, to help make gift baskets), candles (with your colors), designer file folders or journals, etc. Office supply type stores and Christian bookstores are great places to find items marked down. Also shop catalogs and online stores.

Don't forget if you're from a different geographic region, something from your home base makes a nice gift, and you're supporting local businesses. If you are crafty or handy, you can even make small items to offer a personal touch without a lot of expense.

15 CONCERNS SPEAKERS SHARE

Recently I asked public communicators to tell me what their concerns were as a speaker. They really opened up—and began supporting each other through honest and transparent dialogue. I decided to make a list of what they shared and will end with a pep talk to help you, the reader, through your own speaker concerns. If God is for you, who can be against you?

Concerns About Self

- Am I really qualified to do this? I feel like an imposter.

- How do I measure up to other speakers? I fight comparison traps and often feel like I'm not good enough.

- Will I be alert to God's direction for my messages? I want to prepare what he leads and be willing to change it even during the presentation. God knows what the audience needs.

- What if I forget what I want to say and can't find it in my notes? This causes me to panic, which almost blinds me and blurs the words on the page.

- What if I know the heart of my message, but don't convey it well? I know what I want to say, but I'm afraid I might not word it so the audience understands.

Concerns About Business

- How do I set and discuss fees? It's so awkward! Will event planners think it's too high (presuming I'm a diva) or too low (assuming I'm a novice)?

- How will event planners hear about me? I am not good at getting the word out and just wish they'd call already!

- How do I get better organization for my work space, my documents, my calendar, and time management? I feel like things are out of control.

- What if event planners misunderstand something as we're getting the event planned and set up? I think I'm being clear, but there always seems to be communication issues.

- How will I keep my calendar filled? I can't find as many events as I used to because it seems like there are fewer in-person events and more are online or live streaming.

Concerns About Events

- Will the message "land" with the audience and meet their needs? Sometimes I don't get a good read on the audience.

- How will I handle technical glitches during the presentation?

- What if I get asked to fill in for another speaker and have no time to prepare? I'm not good at extemporaneous speaking.

- Will the audience understand the terminology I use, or do I need to figure out new ways to communicate so they get it, without dumbing it down?

- How many books should I take to sell at events? I never know how many to pack, and don't want to run out or have to send books home.

Be real, which of these are concerns to which you relate? Once you figure out what's burdening your heart and overwhelming your mind, you're well on your way to dealing with anything that might be holding you back. You can research answers to your dilemmas once you identify what's bothering you.

What I want to discuss is the core of each concern. Fear. I can pinpoint fear even in some speakers who say they aren't fearful. It's human nature—something we continue to battle as we grow into God's likeness. And it's also a familiar tactic used by the enemy to derail us from achieving the goals God has for us. (He's so predictable!)

Fear causes us to doubt our ability to carry out God's purpose in our lives. It doesn't dilute our passion; it simply sabotages it. One way to overcome fear is to tap in to that purpose and passion regarding your speaking. This helps both your heart and your head reverse the effects of fear.

Fear can paralyze us and keep us from doing what needs done. We neglect taking care of business, because we're uncertain what to do, or if what we do will make a difference. Fear tells us lies and zaps our energy. It causes brain fog. It looks for easy ways out.

Shannon L. Alder says, "Fear is the glue that keeps you stuck. Faith is the solvent that sets you free."

Faith helps you trust God's plan so you can step out in obedience to his direction even when you are afraid you will mess up. Faith says, "I might get it wrong on my own, but as I follow God's direction, I will be closer to getting it right. Knowing God will be with me on my speaking journey helps me remember I have no reason to fear." Faith puts fear in its place, and points to the place God dwells. As you enter that sacred God-place, you will be on solid ground to start dealing with those concerns so you can move forward.

SECTION SEVEN

SPECIAL COMMISSION
Sending Up a Prayer

KEEPING A BIBLICAL FOCUS

M atthew 6:19-33, a paraphrase for communicators:

¹⁹ Don't desire the treasures of this earth, such as selfish success and advancement at any cost. The results from this are temporary at best, and can easily be lost.

²⁰ Store your treasures in heaven, where it really counts for eternity.

²¹ Where you store your treasure reflects your desires and heart-passions.

²² When you are plugged in to God, you have light. When your motives reflect his light, you reflect his glow through your whole body.

²³ But when your motives are selfish, you absorb darkness. And if you think you are reflecting light when you are actually void of light, you deceive yourself!

²⁴ No communicator can serve two masters. For you will hate one and love the other; you will be devoted to one and despise the other. You cannot serve both God and money.

[25] That is why I tell you not to worry about everyday life—whether you have sharp speaker promo materials and catchy topics. Whether you gain book contracts and book sales. Whether you receive media interviews and speaking engagements. Isn't life more than this?

[26] God takes care of all creation. Aren't you far more valuable to him than the rest of creation?

[27] Can all your worries about speaking and writing add a single breath to your life?

[28] And why worry about your success? If God makes temporary creations, such as the flowers shine for all around to see, why would he not help you to shine?

[29] Even Solomon in all his glory couldn't outshine the glorious fields.

[30] If God cares so much about temporary things, like wildflowers, he certainly cares for what matters to you. Because you matter to him. Why do you have so little faith?

[31] So don't worry about these things, saying, "What will I write? Where will I speak? What media will interview me?"

[32] These things dominate the thoughts of unbelieving communicators, but your heavenly father already knows all your needs.

[33] Seek the Kingdom of God above all else, and live righteously, and he will give you everything you need, especially those desires of your heart that align with his good purpose for your life.

Glossary

Deliverable: a measurable outcome or end result promised in promotional materials or a contract.

E-blast: A mailer, usually originating from an online program that provides templates and services to help you create mailing lists and mailers. Often you can track and study results after you send out the e-blast.

Green Room: The anteroom adjacent to a TV stage for relaxation before or after a guest is on air.

Lagniappe: An unexpected bonus. Something extra.

Marketing: The action or business of promoting and selling products or services. In a broader sense, in selling a brand or a person.

Media Outlet: The specific media station or program engaged by publicity efforts.

Promotion: Activity that produces awareness or spreads the word in a way that brings additional exposure.

Publicity: Exposure via the media, such as radio, television, print publications and online.

Pull Quote: A brief attention-grabbing quotation, typically in a distinct typeface, taken from the main text of an article and used for a subheading or graphic feature, like a text box. Also called a call out or box quote.

Rider: A list of expectations the speaker asks the host to supply in order to do the event, included in a contract.

Turnkey Event: A pre-planned event to allow the host to have a ready-made (instant) program. Event planners can use this package to develop a full event without the hassle. It might include: skits, menus, recipes, decoration ideas, songs, promo materials, and more.

Value-Added: Plans to deliver increased return on investment—bonus goods or services or some other benefit or perk.

Voice: A person's point of view, perspective, style, branding, outlook, goals, and mission—all rolled up into one. It is as distinctive as a fingerprint.

Wii-FM: What's In It For Me (the go-to phrase of most consumers).

Acknowledgements

I've had so many people and groups influence my development as a communicator. "Thank you" seems inadequate, but is certainly heartfelt to:

Mom (Wanona Lamb Carlton). You were the first to realize I was destined to be a communicator. I'm certain I wore you down with my fluent and prolific talking, starting at an early age. You raised me with the understanding that I could do just about anything I set my mind to.

CLASSEMINARS. Thanks to my family at CLASS who invested time and knowledge into my career. A special thanks to: Florence Littauer, Gerry Wakeland, Betty Southard, Linda Gilden, Tama Westman and Karen Porter. Your confidence in the work God started in me is continuing to breathe life into my calling as a speaker.

My wisdom team. You support me with your notes, calls, prayers and wise words. Many have prayed for me, but several have gone above and beyond when it comes to support. Special acknowledgement goes to: Michelle Cox, Michelle Rayburn, Joanie Shawhan, Stephenie Hovland, Jessica Caudill, Robin Steinweg, Erin Eddings, Gina Stinson, and Sarah Wisor.

WordGirls. I've had a blast creating a membership-based community of female Christian writers who love fiddling with words as much as I do. You fuel me.

Lin Johnson, for seeing the potential I had in equipping speakers with these helpful industry tools. You recruited me to write the public speaking column for Christian Communicator, and then gave me the nudge to consider writing a book for speakers. This book is a result of your recommendation. Thank you for seeing the potential!

Joy Weese Moll, my writing buddy. Our virtual Writing Bee sessions spur me on to keep writing when it would be easier to procrastinate. Thank you for the added accountability and the fun way to "do" writing.

My faith family at Praise Church. Getting filled up weekly assures I don't run dry. Thanks to my spiritual leaders: Reg Lloyd and Mike Arnold. I'm grateful for a mentorship relationship with Tammy Arrington. I'm especially connected at the heart to our small group. Thanks for keeping it real.

My friend and copyeditor, Robin Steinweg. Thank you for being my biggest cheerleader and prayer warrior. Your edits and feedback sharpen me and improve my books. Now it's time for you to use the book in launching your own speaking ministry!

Virginia Smith and her editorial team at Next Step Books, for editing *Speaker to Speaker*, the book that evolved into *The Ultimate Speaker's Guide*. Thank you for believing in this project and publishing the original book baby. I was sad when NSB closed its doors. I hope you are pleased in this rebirth of the project and all the new material we added.

My indie publishing consultant and book designer, Michelle Rayburn. You not only showed me the ropes, you adeptly jumped them to make sure I had a quality end product. I'm proud of my book baby, but even more proud to call you friend.

My beloved husband, Russ. Thanks for your devoted support as I pursue God's goals for me as a communicator. You have been my role model in the public speaking arena, with your powerful messages and lessons over the years. By rough calculation, you've delivered at least 3500 public addresses since we entered the ministry. You're incredible.

Father, Son and Spirit. Father, your love gives me something to talk about. Jesus, your life gives me an example to follow. Holy Spirit, your presence gives me wisdom and peace. Thank you for sending me out as a communicator and giving me opportunities to help other speakers and writers shine as they reflect your glory.

About the Author

Kathy **Carlton Willis** spins many plates as writer, speaker and platform coach. She has acquired a resource kit full of tips, tools, and takeaways for speakers and is frequently invited to coach speakers one-on-one and at seminars. She is the speaker columnist for *The Christian Communicator* and is a contributing author for *The Reason We Speak*, previously published by Proverbs 31 ministries.

Others consider Kathy a guru for speakers. She also has created think tanks for businesses, civic groups and even a city manager and mayor. She is invited to speak to civic, church and non-profit groups on motivational and inspirational topics. One of her big loves is to help people brainstorm, and then motivate them when they feel stuck, so they know where they're headed and how to get there.

Kathy writes and speaks with a balance of funny and faith—whimsy and wisdom. She's adept at coaching speakers from a Christian worldview, equipped with a Bible degree coupled with industry knowledge. She is simply known as "God's Grin Gal." Over a thousand of Kathy's articles have been published in books, magazines, newspapers and online publications. Her Bible study, *Grin with Grace*, debuted her "Grin" brand. CBN (Christian Broadcasting Network) features her popular devo-study *Grin and Grow with Kathy*.

Kathy has a background in newspaper journalism, working as copyeditor and feature writer for several newspapers. She served as grammar and style guru for three publications—red ink is her friend! She is also an expert in author promotion, having served as literary publicist for over 200 popular authors and publishing houses.

She's a contributing writer for *Upgrade Your Life*, and has archived articles with *The Christian Pulse, My Purpose Now, The Pastor's Wife Speaks*, and others.

Kathy graduated with honors from Bible College, holding degrees in Bible and Church Education, and served for over thirty years in fulltime church ministry with her pastor/husband, Russ.

Kathy works with women's groups and writers' groups, inside and outside the church. She enjoys coaching others to learn how to remove the training wheels and not just risk, but take pleasure in the joy ride of a life trusting in God.

Learn more at Kathy's website: **kathycarltonwillis.com**